A MOUNTAIN MOVING FAITH

Teaching Young People to Reach the Ultimate Summit

A MOUNTAIN MOVING FAITH

Teaching Young People to Reach the Ultimate Summit

Matthew W. Morine

GOSPEL
ADVOCATE
A TRUSTED NAME SINCE 1855

Published by Gospel Advocate Co.
1006 Elm Hill Pike, Nashville, TN 37210
www.gospeladvocate.com

ISBN: 978-0-89225-659-4

Dedication

*This book is dedicated to my parents,
Doug and Joyce Morine,
who always believed in me when others
doubted my abilities.*

TABLE OF CONTENTS

Acknowledgments

Most successful men are married to even more successful women. Opinions on how we measure success might vary, but rest assured the success a man is blessed with is often the result of "marrying up," as they say. I am such a man. It should be acknowledged that all of the accomplishments God has provided me started on that day when my wife, Charity, said yes to this project of a man. She has stood by my side in every goal, dream and success God has given us. This book would never exist without her constant love for me.

Also, I would like to thank three teenagers who helped read the manuscript and provided invaluable comments: Bethany Moore, Hope Schmalzried and Kaitlyn Rodriguez. These ladies provided insights from a teen mind and helped the book be better in every way.

This book was also finished because of the best editor ever, who helped me with the first manuscript. Jena Webb has been a blessing to work with, and she transformed me from a terrible writer to a great one. Thank you so much.

Finally, this book would never have seen print if not for my friend Gregory Alan Tidwell, editor of *Gospel Advocate* magazine, who always encouraged this project. It was his belief in me that made a huge difference in my life. For being a simple Midwestern preacher, he has provided a wonderful impact on the church and my life.

Foreword

You never know what you'll see at the top of a mountain. One I will never forget is Machu Picchu, near Cusco, Peru. Deep in the Peruvian jungle lies an ancient Incan village that has likely been deserted for 500 years. The incredible complex, much of it built on a steep slope, spans five acres and boasts beautiful terraces, 3,000 steps and 150 structures, including a temple for sun worship. Was it a royal palace? Maybe it was a religious site? Some think it might have been a prison complex. Whatever it was, it is amazing to find this incredible site 2,400 feet above sea level in a tropical mountain forest on the slopes of the Peruvian Andes deep in the continent of South America. The journey from my home to the center of this ancient mountaintop city involved 2½ hours by car, 10½ hours by plane (three flights), 1½ hours by taxi, 3+ hours by train, 30 minutes by bus and about 15 minutes by foot. The Incas did not have mechanized tools or modern modes of transportation. How did these ancient architects and builders do it? I don't know – but they did.

As my fingers rest poised above the keys to my MacBook, my mind places me on a contemplative peak, gazing down on modern society. I survey a collision of cultures, religions and philosophies as humanity wrestles with post-postmodernism, religious wars (intellectual and actual), information overload, instant communication with lessening personal contact, and the age-old struggle to treat all people of all races, genders and nationalities with kindness and love. How does a person come to faith in this context? How do we climb to the spiritual heights God has envisioned for us? Matthew Morine seeks to help us answer those questions. Having studied with Matt in graduate school, I know that he is a competent scholar, a diligent student of the biblical text and a passionate proclaimer of God's inspired message. He combines those tools with his mountain-climbing experiences to give us some tips that can help in our spiritual journeys. Matthew calls us to live by faith, not an ordinary faith, but a faith that can move mountains. It will not be easy, but it can be done. We have the Word of God to guide us, amazing people to travel with us and an awesome God to empower us. Strap up your boots, lift your packs, fill your water bottles, open your Bibles and come climb with us. You never know what you will see at the top of a mountain.

W. Kirk Brothers
Assistant Professor of Bible
Freed-Hardeman University
Henderson, Tenn.

Introduction

This book is about faith and fourteeners. What is a fourteener? It is a mountain over 14,000 feet, a term well known in Colorado, where the most popular hobbies are hiking and climbing. There are 58 mountains in Colorado over 14,000 feet. The tallest is Mount Elbert at 14,440 or 14,439 feet, and the shortest is Sunshine Peak at 14,001 feet. Height, however, does not determine the difficulty of climbing these mountains. There is a rating system from class one, which involves a trail to the **summit** (bolded words throughout the book are included in the glossary), to class five, which is vertical rock climbing. Most of the fourteeners range from class two to four and include rocky trails and climbing with thousands of feet of **exposure**. Typically, this is done without a rope, which, I can say from personal experience, certainly helps your prayer life.

After five years, driving thousands of miles, hiking countless hours, not to mention a huge amount of dedication, I have climbed 54 of the 58 peaks. Climbing to the top of a peak is a grueling process. You either camp in the middle of nowhere or wake up at 1 a.m. to reach a **trailhead** by daybreak. Sometimes you hike for more than 12 hours straight, climbing over 7,000 vertical feet in a single day. At numerous times you ask yourself why you are putting your mind and body through the rigors of climbing. You often feel like quitting, but instead, you persevere. You push yourself to reach the summit and earn the satisfaction of standing thousands of feet above the world.

Climbing fourteeners is very similar to developing faith. Growing in your faith is not always easy. Moving from a teen to adulthood is a difficult journey too. Countless hours of study, dedication to service and overcoming various obstacles are all necessary to reach the ultimate summit of heaven. Faith is not for the faint of heart. It requires you to make choices that are not always simple and straightforward, choices that will dictate your actions and goals. During the teenage years, you will make choices that will forever change the path you take, for example who your friends are, where you go to college, who you date and what you will study. It is easier to sleep in my comfortable bed than in a freezing cold tent, but then I would never achieve the triumph of reaching unimaginable heights. I could attend service without giving to my community or brethren in Christ, but then I would never obtain the glory of salvation. As a teen, you can take the easy path of video games, avoiding homework and going along with the crowd, but the greatest feelings will come from those challenges that pushed you to your limit.

A great feeling of accomplishment comes from standing on top of a mountain, gazing down on the world. Imagine how much greater it will be to hear God say to you, "Well done, good and faithful servant." The development of faith is a worthy and satisfying task, but it takes work. It is an upward battle with many seen and unseen obstacles, but you will not fight it alone. God is always with you. This book will help remind you how to find Him every day. It will assist you in reaching your goal of being found faithful in the eyes of God. This book will help secure your faith during a time in which the world will be trying to destroy your soul. It will help you to attain the ultimate mountain of all: heaven.

1

Mountain-Moving Faith

Matthew 17:14-20

Let's be honest: the Bible can be hard to understand sometimes. It not only gives us a list of answers for daily issues or a table of do's and don'ts but also provides verses of metaphors and parables from which we unearth advice. On top of that, some of the stories seem totally impossible, and God's promises appear too fantastic to be true. So we ignore them, refusing to believe any of it, credible or not, because it's easier to not care than to search for truth. Developing your personal faith is a challenge.

What if we dealt with everything this way? Should we quit a sport because training is too hard? Or stop playing an instrument because we have to practice? Should we drop out of school because we don't want to study? Should we stop meeting new people, making friends or dating simply because it requires effort? No. We should persevere and seek to improve ourselves in order to achieve the highest level of success possible. It's the same with faith. We must practice and strengthen our faith through action and understanding. We need to work at our relationship with God and believe that He is truly present in all things. In this way, we can achieve success in life and the infinite reward of salvation. With the smallest grain of faith, we may move mountains.

But how? How do we move a mountain with nothing more than belief? How can we strengthen something we can't see or comprehend? It sounds idealistic, being able to move a mountain. As a mountain climber, I can tell you that at times I have dreamed of bringing the peak closer, making the climb easier or my legs stronger. Looking up at a mountain 14,000 feet tall is daunting and more than a little bit alarming, especially if you think of all the things that could go wrong while trying to conquer it. Despite all my hoping, I know the mountain isn't going to change to suit me. It is what it is, and I must adapt if I am ever going to reach the summit. It's either go big or go home.

We all have mountains, obstacles we need to overcome. It could be stress from your parents at home, bullies who won't leave you alone at school or the youth group that is more about cliques than Christ. We want an easy fix, but we know that time and effort are required to solve problems. Why, then, do we not give God the same understanding? We have hundreds of problems in our day-to-day lives that we wish would go away with a simple prayer. We want that mountain of difficulty to disappear, but when nothing happens from prayer, we blame God for abandoning us, for failing us. But who is ignoring whom? We ask God to prove that He is there, but we never prove to Him that we believe. We fear disappointment. We fear placing our trust in God. We become too busy, distracted or lazy to strengthen our relationship with Him. Because of this, we end up encountering suffering and pain. So I ask: how can we expect Him to do for us what we are not willing to do for Him?

Matthew 17:14-20

14 And when they came to the crowd, a man came up to [Jesus] and, kneeling before him,

15 said, "Lord, have mercy on my son, for he is an epileptic and he suffers terribly. For often he falls into the fire, and often into the water.

16 "And I brought him to your disciples, and they could not heal him."

17 And Jesus answered, "O faithless and twisted generation, how long am I to be with you? How long am I to bear with you? Bring him here to me."

18 And Jesus rebuked the demon, and it came out of him, and the boy was healed instantly.

19 Then the disciples came to Jesus privately and said, "Why could we not cast it out?"

20 He said to them, "Because of your little faith. For truly, I say to you, if you have faith like a grain of mustard seed, you will say to this mountain, 'Move from here to there,' and it will move, and nothing will be impossible for you."

It's a sad story, one of the pain and desperation of a father to save his son. There is no greater pain for a parent than to watch, helplessly, as a child suffers. This poor father had already gone to the disciples seeking aid, only to have his hope challenged when they were unable to change his son's condition. Did he quit then? Did he accept that his son would continue to suffer and possibly die a horrible death because he could do nothing? Of course not. He had faith and the will to challenge his own doubts by seeking out Christ.

Firm Faith

Faith gave the man strength to persevere. Despite the struggle, he sought a solution and refused to accept failure. This is the moment of truth when faith is tested, and we must either leap forward or remain behind. The man tried everything, searched for every possible answer, and exhausted all his options only to come face to face with failure again and again. Yet his faith remained strong and constant. He knew the power of God could save his son.

What would you have done in his position? What lengths would you have gone to in order to save your loved ones? Years ago, my daughter suffered extreme eczema that covered her entire body. It might not sound as severe as epileptic seizures, but for a child, it's just as traumatic. It started in the normal places, the folds of the arms and legs, before spreading to the top of her head. The worst part was the eczema that broke out on her face. At times she looked as if she had been severely burned. People would comment on it, asking what had happened and what was wrong, all of which embarrassed her terribly. Most nights she struggled to sleep, waking up constantly to scratch until she bled. It was awful for her. Her mother and I struggled because we were unable to help. We tried everything. We went to doctors, naturalists and every website that promised to heal eczema. Nothing worked. It was a never-ending cycle of hope followed by disappointment, and all the while my little girl was in pain.

After a while you begin to ask yourself what you are doing. Why do you keep trying? Children with eczema can grow out of it and be fine as adults, but did I want to let her suffer all that time because I could not handle the disappointment? Did the man described by Matthew want his son to continue suffering simply because he had not found an easy solution? No. And even though Christ's disciples were unable to help, he still believed their Teacher could do something. He still held on to hope.

Hope Strengthens

Love for his son and God reaffirmed the father's belief and hope that he could move his personal mountain. Sure enough, Jesus healed the man's son but rebuked His own followers. He called them "faithless and twisted" (Matthew 17:17); the fact that they could not heal the sick boy proved they did not have a true, strong belief in Jesus yet.

Christ's disappointment is understandable. His disciples saw His works and witnessed miracles beyond the average person's understanding. But they were unable to heal the boy because, for them, seeing was not believing. They were "twisted," corrupted by the world around them, which had blinded them to the true glory of God. The man who lived with the torturous suffering of his son exhibited greater faith than the very disciples who followed Jesus.

Everyone deals with these moments of shaken or lost faith because, bottom line, faith is hard. It could be that one of your peers was killed in a car wreck, or you witness a leader in the youth group succumb to sin. These times demand a great deal of trust, commitment and understanding, all without obvious or immediate results. When climbing a mountain, I have to put a lot of faith into the durability of my gear, the strength of my body, and the people with whom I am climbing. I am not embarrassed to admit that some moments are downright scary. Will the **ledge** hold my weight? Will my hands slip when they grab the next **handhold**? Are my arms strong enough to help me up?

We were climbing Crestone Needle, a 14,000-foot peak in the Sangre de Cristo **Range**, and I needed to cross from one gully to another. There was a large separation between the two – too wide to step over. It was close enough that only a decent jump could get you across. In most circumstances, you would not think twice about this type of jump when you're on the ground. Add a few hundred feet of open air beneath you, and the situation changes drastically. Of course, I didn't want to jump. There was nothing to catch me if I miscalculated my body's ability to get me across. Even though I saw others leap over it before me, I had a moment where I second-guessed myself. My friend Nick gave me the incentive. All it took was three little words: "Go for it." So I did. I approached the gap and made my legs push off and propel my body so that I landed safely on the other side. I have confidence in my abilities, and I have climbed enough that I have honed the skills needed to do so successfully. But sometimes we all need a little push to go that one step further, that one level higher.

We have all heard the phrase "a leap of faith." That is what I took, literally. I had to trust in myself and my ability to get across that gap. It is the same with faith in God. We need to trust in Him, to trust that He is there for us and that He will help us in our many "leaps" throughout life. Each time you trust, each time you jump, you strengthen your faith in the Lord.

Doubt Weakens

In Matthew's account, the disciples attempted to cast out the demon. When they failed, they asked Christ why, to which He replied: "Because of your little faith" (Matthew 17:20). The disciples "leaped," but proved they were too weak in faith to land safely on the other side. Moreover, the disciples asked Christ the wrong question. They asked why they weren't successful, not why

19

their faith was weak. They weren't seeking to improve themselves or strengthen their belief; they wanted only to achieve the glory represented by Christ. They wanted the power but not the work.

The disciples saw Jesus perform miracles, but they did not understand how it was done. Christ chastised them for their misunderstanding by saying that the smallest amount of faith, a mustard seed's worth, was all that was required to accomplish great things. The metaphor of moving a mountain illustrated how just a little faith was needed to perform miracles. Yet the disciples lacked the faith needed to perform or even understand the miracles.

This is timid faith. We believe in God as long as everything is going well; if we are content, we do not question God's power and knowledge. These circumstances make it easy to have faith in God. What happens when something goes wrong? What do we think when life becomes uncertain, threatening or out of control? We say God has abandoned us, forsaken us or forgotten us. We turn from Him like children throwing a tantrum, refusing to give Him our continued trust because all is not as we wish. When life is great, faith is strong, but when life becomes difficult, as it often does, our belief weakens and we turn away from God's eternal love.

Trials and tribulations shake our faith. It's not uncommon for many teens to lose their connection with God after going to college. Contrary to what you might believe, your parents likely do everything within their power to help you avoid temptation and other negative circumstances. They shelter and protect you, giving you time to fortify your own faith. When you move away from home, you no longer have the same support system or spiritual reinforcements as before. The independence provided in college allows you to discover who you are as an individual, but it can also overwhelm you. This is the first time you will be free to do as you wish without parental supervision; excess is all too often the result.

All decisions, however, have consequences. Partying, drinking and focusing on your social life cannot strengthen your relationship with God. These vices only lead you down a far darker path and away from true faith in the Lord. The disciples had to develop their own faith to cast out a demon just as we have to develop our own faith to handle the challenges of life. College is an important time of growth in an individual's life. It's the beginning of our adult lives, the moment when we begin to see ourselves as individuals and choose what we want to be when we grow up. It's also a time of testing. As we grow, God watches us; He sees into our hearts and knows us inside and out. We're tested to see how strong our faith is and if, when difficulties arise, we're capable of continuing along the righteous path.

Faith Conquers

True faith can bend without breaking in the most powerful winds and survive the worst trials. It can accomplish anything because it is supported by the almighty power of God. We need only the smallest amount of faith, no more than a mustard seed's worth, and we can move the mightiest of mountains. How apt that Christ used the mustard seed in His analogy, for not only is it the smallest of seeds – reaching only one to two millimeters in diameter – but it also grows into the largest of herbs. Beginning with this miniscule amount, we can strengthen our faith, hone our understanding of God's power to work in the world, and reach previously insurmountable heights.

Jesus used the mustard seed and mountain metaphor to inspire His disciples, who continued to struggle with what God asked of them. They witnessed Christ's miracles and the glory of God all around them but did not fully understand its importance. Everyone must allow his or her faith to grow and mature. It's not instantaneous. It takes the dedication of the mind and soul to realize its potential. However, no matter how small it begins, once strengthened, faith will enable you to do the impossible, all through the power of God.

What is it you want? What do you seek when you look to God for help? Do you want to conquer the mountain and achieve something great, something remarkable? Or do you want to quit and watch life pass you by? It's easy enough for me to quote Scripture and relate stories from the time of Christ, but what does this mean in our day-to-day lives? If these men, these disciples who hung around with Jesus Christ, had doubts, it only makes sense that we would too. Knowing that they struggled with their faith means that we are not alone with our doubts. The question is how do we deal with them? How do we grow that grain of faith? How do we know when we have it?

In our current "show me" culture in which science and evidence reign, it's difficult to believe in an untouchable, divine Being. It's even more difficult to maintain such faith when faced with life's challenges. A person being bullied in school is sure to question the Lord's presence when the bullies never face punishment. But He is there. In the victim's community, friends, family and church, the Lord is always there, providing support in the times when the victim is too weak to defend himself. Similarly, God strengthens others to speak out against the abuse because they too follow the principles of Christ, though they might be unaware of it. Whoever speaks out against injustice or defends the weak, whoever refuses to raise his hand in violence after violence is done to him, his heart is pure and open to the Lord's glory. His actions are the seeds of faith and the first steps toward moving the mountain.

Discussion Questions

1. In Matthew 17:14-16, what was the father's motivation for approaching Jesus? What is your motivation for approaching Jesus? What calls you to strengthen your faith?

2. In Matthew 17:17-18, Jesus had some strong opinions about His generation and the time in which they were living. What words did He use to describe them? Do these same words apply to the present generation? If so, what lesson should we take from this story?

3. Based on the story from Matthew 17:19-20, how large does your faith need to be to move mountains? What steps can you take to develop a mountain-moving faith?

4. What are some obstacles that one must overcome when developing a mountain-moving faith today? What are some obstacles you have had to face in developing your faith?

CLIMBING 101

Mountains

Did you know that the famous song "America the Beautiful" was inspired by a Colorado fourteener? In 1893, Katharine Lee Bates, an English teacher at Wellesley College in Massachusetts, agreed to take a summer teaching position at Colorado College in Colorado Springs, Colo. During her 2,000-mile train trip through the metropolis of Chicago, the prairies of Kansas and into Colorado, Bates was inspired by the beauty and vastness of the United States. During her stay in Colorado, she and others rode a prairie wagon up Pike's Peak. Near the top they had to leave the wagon and go the rest of the way on mules. It was this trip up the mountain that inspired her famous song.

O beautiful, for spacious skies,
For amber waves of grain,
For purple mountain majesties
Above the fruited plain!

The Colorado fourteeners have inspired countless men and women throughout the years. These majestic peaks can inspire awe and humility, as well as adventure and faith, but only for those who are willing to embark on the journey to the summit.

2

Test or Trust
Matthew 16:5-11

Ropes are important tools in mountain climbing. Not all the fourteeners in Colorado require them, but there are a few places where a rope would really come in handy. There's a steep **downgrade** on North Maroon, for example, that would be easier if you **anchored** into a rock and **rappelled** off rather than going straight down the **rock face**. In snow or slippery conditions, having a rope to connect you to someone else can mean greater security against injury. If one person slips, the connecting rope anchors you to the other person, catching you before you fall.

The Hourglass, a steep downgrade on Little Bear Peak, is the most notorious section on the fourteeners that necessitates a rope. The Hourglass is famous for two reasons: the rock fall and its sheer steepness. The shape of the mountain funnels all and any loose rock down the edge of the Hourglass, making it an even more treacherous climb. At the top of the Hourglass is an anchor with a rope attached. Throughout the year, hikers use it to rappel down the sheer rock face, avoiding the more challenging task of finding handholds and ledges in the rock. This rope, however, is left in the elements for long periods of time, not to mention the wear and tear from climbers who use it. It can fray, split or lose its strength in a variety of ways.

When this rope is all that stands between you and a dangerous fall, you want to be able to trust in its durability and support. If the rope is weak in any way, it's likely to give out the minute you let it take your weight. This is why most people still **descend** the old-fashioned way, ignoring the rope and its questionable reliability except in an emergency. The rope is changed from time to time to avoid any accidents, but this does not guarantee safety. A friend of mine once heard that the rope had been replaced and decided to take advantage quickly, climbing Little Bear Peak shortly thereafter. When preparing to use the rope, however, he noticed two cuts in it. Natural cuts or not, I am not sure I would entrust my life to the new rope's questionable integrity.

Matthew 16:5-11

5 When the disciples reached the other side, they had forgotten to bring any bread.

6 Jesus said to them, "Watch and beware of the leaven of the Pharisees and Sadducees."

7 And they began discussing it among themselves, saying, "We brought no bread."

8 But Jesus, aware of this, said, "O you of little faith, why are you discussing among yourselves the fact that you have no bread?

9 "Do you not yet perceive? Do you not remember the five loaves for the five thousand, and how many baskets you gathered?

10 "Or the seven loaves for the four thousand, and how many baskets you gathered?

11 "How is it that you fail to understand that I did not speak about bread? Beware of the leaven of the Pharisees and Sadducees."

Trust is never an easy thing to come by, particularly when it is trusting in another person. When people questioned Jesus and His teachings, they were acting as normal humans with normal skepticism. They believed in something better, something greater than what they saw around them in first-century Israel. It was Jesus who cast the rope down the mountain, calling His brothers and sisters of faith to climb closer to God. Just as with the rope on the Hourglass, people questioned the integrity of this rope. Some tested it and found they had confidence in its strength; others refused to put any trust in it and struggled along without the Lord's support.

Trust is a common theme in the New Testament because doubt is a natural human instinct. We want proof that something exists, proof as to why this is false but that is true. In order to learn, we question. Would Christ have needed to perform miracles if no one had doubted? Jesus was tested by the people of His time, both His followers and critics; the stories of the Bible were recorded so that the doubt of those who read them would decrease. The truth would forever lie before them – evidence of Christ's divinity and our future salvation. In these accounts are people who questioned Jesus and His teaching but who were answered with truth: Jesus Christ is the Son of God and the source of our salvation.

In Matthew 16, the Pharisees and Sadducees demanded a sign from heaven that would prove Jesus was the Christ. Once more, the disciples' doubt and distrust of Jesus blinded them to the multitude of miracles He had already performed. He healed the sick and fed thousands, but they still refused to see His glory. Danger was in their continued, willful blindness. The Pharisees and Sadducees held positions of influence within the community; they had the ability to sway others from the truth of God's glory. It was this power Jesus warned His disciples of when He said, "Watch and beware of the leaven of the Pharisees and Sadducees" (v. 6).

Confused, the disciples explained they had forgotten to bring bread with them. Christ replied, "How is it that you fail to understand that I did not speak about bread?" (Matthew 16:11). You can almost imagine Jesus rolling His eyes at this point. He was using a metaphor. How many times had He proved Himself to His followers and they still misunderstood? He had no need for bread to be able to feed the multitudes. The leaven was a metaphor for doctrine, and the Pharisees and Sadducees were sources of bad doctrine. When Christ warned against their leaven, He intended to warn against doubt and ignorance.

Examining the Rope

The Pharisees and Sadducees never trusted in the rope provided by Christ. They didn't want to see proof of Jesus' divinity but sought to mock Him. Like bullies at school, they ridiculed His efforts and turned a blind eye to any form of success. It didn't matter what He did or said because the Pharisees and Sadducees never believed Jesus was the Christ. They questioned God in ignorance without the desire to be educated toward stronger faith. The disciples, however, had the luxury of choice.

The disciples were faced with two options: listen to Christ or follow in the tradition of the Pharisees and Sadducees. Would they listen to the people with earthly power or follow Jesus on the path to an eternal reward? After all Jesus had done, some doubt was still among even the most loyal of His followers. Moreover, they misunderstood Him. He had warned them to beware the leaven or teaching of the Pharisees and Sadducees, which produced a panic about forgetting to bring bread with them on their trip. When I imagine their reaction, it seems almost comical. "Did you bring it?" "No, I thought he did." "He didn't bring it." "Well, I didn't bring it!" "I brought the water; no one told me to bring bread!" And all the while Jesus was standing there, rubbing His brow in amazement and frustration – mostly frustration.

Their first thought was of bodily needs – their need for food – but never the needs of the soul. This was what Christ was warning them against. The Pharisees and Sadducees, among others, were not fighting for the salvation of mankind. Their work among the community was temporary and earth-bound, but Jesus looked to heaven and the eternal salvation of the soul. He warned them against following false leadership by reminding them of what He had already provided. Jesus fed over 4,000 people by multiplying seven loaves of bread and a few small fish (Matthew 15:32-38). His disciples were there. They witnessed this miraculous and divine gift; they saw for themselves the glory of the Lord and His Son. Why, then, were they afraid of being without a meager amount of bread?

The multiplication of the loaves and fish is a well-known miracle. It was a sign of divine intervention, just like the sign asked for by the

Pharisees and Sadducees in Matthew 16. Christ explained to them, "When it is evening, you say, 'It will be fair weather, for the sky is red.' And in the morning, 'It will be stormy today, for the sky is red and threatening.' You know how to interpret the appearance of the sky, but you cannot interpret the signs of the times" (Matthew 16:2-3). Each day, the people saw the glories of God. Each day, they denied these gifts as divine in origin. This is what Christ was warning His disciples to avoid. They had seen His power in feeding the hungry from limited supplies but forgot it just as easily. There was no consistency in their faith, no confidence in what Jesus taught them.

In rock climbing, a terrifying moment comes between letting go of the rock and rappelling down. Climbing up, you trust in your abilities; you can measure your strength and confidence and sense when you are growing tired or reaching the point of exhaustion. Climbing up, you do not need to rely as heavily on the rope or other equipment, even if it is there for safety. Only after you reach your goal do you need to give serious thought to the security of your gear. As a responsible climber, you rely on your own tried and tested equipment, approved by other users and guaranteed by multiple organizations to withstand the harshest elements. It's assured to hold your weight and bring you safely to the ground, but all of these promises do little to erase your fear of falling.

My son, Noah, loves to climb. When he reaches the top, I tell him when to let go because I am below connected to him by ropes and ready to **belay** him down safely. Does he let go? Nope. He clings to the rock, refusing to trust the rope and, in part, me. This is natural. A rope is such a simple thing, made by someone you will probably never meet. You are not only trusting in the quality of the rope but also in the quality of the person and company that commissioned it. What we must remember is that this is their job. Do you distrust the police because you do not know them all individually? No, you believe that they will continue to uphold the law and keep you safe because that is their job. Faith is no different. We trust that Christ sacrificed Himself for our redemption; we trust that God is with us always, watching and protecting us because this is what the Father and Son do. These are their "jobs."

Trusting the Rope

In Matthew 16, the disciples were confused because they were not sure what they did wrong. Why did Jesus warn them against the leaven of the Pharisees and Sadducees? Why was He disappointed in them? Meanwhile, Jesus wondered how His followers could be so blind. How could they think He was talking about the absence of food when He could produce it at will? He reminded them of His miracle with the loaves for the 5,000 and 4,000 because they seemed to have forgotten His gifts (vv. 9-11). He fed thousands of people from almost nothing, but His disciples were panicking about their lunch. This didn't portray total trust in the Lord, but lingering doubt, which, according to Christ, was caused by the false teaching of the Pharisees and Sadducees.

The disciples had taken the preliminary step toward accepting Jesus as the Christ but had not made the leap toward trusting His promises. They straddled the line of faith, refusing to take that final step and put themselves wholly before the Lord. These men were accustomed to listening to the Pharisees and Sadducees as well as other leaders in the Jewish community. It was almost habit. When these same leaders, who were accepted as wise men, questioned Jesus and His promises, they sent messages of doubt into the community. Jesus never deterred His followers from asking questions; in fact, He promoted looking at the world in a new, revolutionary way. He demanded rational thought, not blind allegiance. All around us is the work of God's labors; Jesus asks only that we observe these glories and acknowledge the One who made them.

Decide for Yourself

The choice left to Christ's companions – to follow either Him or the Pharisees – isn't so different from the choice we have today. There are many religions in this world, and everyone has an opinion on which is right or wrong, better or worse, true or false. You're going to come across many people who don't believe in Christ's divinity, who doubt He existed at all. Some of these nonbelievers might be your friends, teachers and people in your community you have known your whole life. Not everyone will be vocal about his or her beliefs, but some will argue against Christ and question your faith, just like the Pharisees and Sadducees. This might sound strange, but listen to them. Listen to what they believe and what they doubt because only then will you be able to educate them. It's easy to argue blindly, but true understanding arises only from listening and learning.

The Lord gave us free will to strengthen our faith and build it to greater heights. He wants you to willingly come to Him with an open and loving heart, not because you are forced. This, unfortunately, means that, at moments, your faith will be tested and challenged. As we grow, we are exposed to new ideas and beliefs; this can be wonderful but also threatening. We must transition from childhood, where we think our elders are always right, to the real world, where age no longer implies wisdom. In college, you will take courses required by the school that are outside your area of interest or expertise. You have to enter these classes with trust, hoping your teacher knows the subject and will share it in an unbiased way. What if you disagree with something taught? What if the lessons say what you believe is wrong? Are you allowed to question their authority? Teachers have degrees, experience and age on their side. What right do you have to doubt their leaven?

You have every right. Someone's expertise does not mean he or she is faultless. There will always be questions that make you rethink your faith; do not fear these moments, but embrace them. People will demand proof of God's existence and Jesus' divinity; they will try to fill you with doubt because they are unable to see the glory of the Lord. The disciples panicked over the forgotten bread because they did not have strong faith. They listened to false teaching and weak leadership and refused to see what was right before them. Christ reminded His disciples to trust in Him and take hold of His promises because He would not let them down. He demonstrated the truth of His glory and asked nothing more of His followers than what He was willing to give Himself.

Blind faith is a dangerous thing because not everything or everyone who claims to be Christian is in fact Christian. Think about a couple of movies released in 2014. These movies might have good intentions, but it does not mean you must accept everything within them as the truth. The movie *God's Not Dead*, for example, has a good message but ends with a call to the sinner's prayer. To be saved, you must be baptized. There are no examples or commands in the Bible that suggest the sinner's prayer is authorized as a form of conversion or salvation. Moreover, the movie *Noah* takes a biblical story and turns it into a dramatic, shallow fiction that gives a false impression of the Bible. It's not truth, but entertainment. The Pharisees and Sadducees claimed to follow God, but that did not mean everything they taught was truth. You have to search the Scriptures in order to find the Word of God and the truth it shares (Acts 17:11).

Christ left us a rope to cling to on our journey, but not everyone is confident in its integrity. Instead of testing it, they ignore it completely. We want signs to confirm God exists and Jesus is His Son because we are afraid. What if the rope is weak and breaks? What if someone cuts it and lets us fall? What if there's nothing beyond this life? We all struggle with doubt. We all wonder about faith. But this rope of Christianity is safe and secure. Think about this. Jesus Christ predicted His death, told of the amount of time He would be gone and was raised from the dead. Name one other person in history who died, was buried and was raised again to life? I believe I will trust this man. Here is a man that we still talk about every day, someone who lived more than 2,000 years ago, and He has influenced the entire world. Jesus is trustworthy. He is a secure rope. If you ever become lost, He will be with you to lead you back to safety because He does not need to test you. He has faith in you even when you doubt. He *is* the rope to God and glory. If you trust in Him, Jesus will pull you up and never let you fall.

Discussion Questions

1. In Jesus' warning regarding the Pharisees and Sadducees, what did the bread symbolize?

2. What are some qualities in people that make them trustworthy?

3. Why do you think the disciples were unable to trust Jesus even after witnessing His miracles?

4. Do you trust Jesus? Are there any negatives to trusting or believing in Jesus?

5. Jesus performed many miracles for the faithful, healing and helping those in need. How has Jesus provided for you thus far in your life?

CLIMBING 101

Knots

In rock climbing, there is a certain type of knot used to ensure safety: the figure eight. This particular method of tying off a rope creates a lifeline for the climber. Should a handhold prove unreliable or if a climber slips, the figure eight knot can bear the weight of someone falling. Under this weight the figure eight might jam, but, unlike other knots, it can be more easily undone and not require cutting.

There are some knots that are almost impossible to undo after a fall. The strain they undergo tightens them until they are impossible to undo. So too are certain sins. Once the sinful act has been completed, the consequences cannot always be undone. Although your sin can be forgiven, you will have to live with the results forever.

3

Waves of Trust
Matthew 14:28-33

Not all mountains are created equal. Some have a more distinct shape, like a fin skimming through the clouds. Others look like nothing more than a pile of rocks. Some peaks have defined trails that lead to the summit; a couple might even have paved roads to the top. The fourteeners of Colorado come in all shapes and sizes with a range of difficulty levels: one mountain can be relatively easy, and another, incredibly hard. A class-one peak has, for the most part, a defined trail with no exposure and moderate elevation; class-two peaks are similar, but with slightly rougher terrain. Each class grows progressively harder with greater exposure and wilder landscape until class five, which basically involves climbing up sheer, vertical walls of rock.

The higher the number, the higher the risk, but it is unlikely anyone would start on a class three or four. On the fourteeners, you work your way up. You start on a class one, gaining experience with the easier paths until you are familiar with the physical and mental demands. It is a scary feeling to stand on an exposed ledge, especially without prior experience. I doubt I have to emphasize how unwise it is to attempt a peak you are not prepared to handle. As with life, we begin at a crawl and start to walk only when our bodies and minds are ready to reach new heights.

Matthew 14:28-33

28 And Peter answered him, "Lord, if it is you, command me to come to you on the water."

29 He said, "Come." So Peter got out of the boat and walked on the water and came to Jesus.

30 But when he saw the wind, he was afraid, and beginning to sink he cried out, "Lord, save me."

31 Jesus immediately reached out his hand and took hold of him, saying to him, "O you of little faith, why did you doubt?"

32 And when they got into the boat, the wind ceased.

33 And those in the boat worshiped him, saying, "Truly you are the Son of God."

Sometimes we aren't as prepared as we would like for tackling new elevations. Sometimes we need a little push to let us know we are ready for what is to come and to block out that anxious little voice in the back of our minds. Peter was certainly not ready for the storm erupting around him when he walked on the water with Jesus. The disciples faced great opposition and ridicule from non-believers. Christ's teachings were revolutionary and raised a great deal of concern among the people of the time; fear of change and the unknown meant that the faith of the disciples was constantly brought into question. Being aware of this external pressure, Jesus sought to give His followers lessons that would strengthen their resolve and reaffirm their faith.

One such instance appears in the Gospel of Matthew. Jesus set His disciples in a boat that would sail across the sea during inclement winds. As the waves tossed them about and the wind threatened to capsize the boat, their faith began to falter. When Jesus reappeared, standing on the water, He attempted to comfort them. In their doubt, they feared Him to be a ghost until He calmed them, but even then, doubt remained. Only Christ could command the storm to subside, and Peter asked Jesus to summon him out onto the water.

This wasn't the first time Christ was faced with a violent sea (Matthew 8:23-27), and, as before, His disciples probably expected Him to demonstrate His power by calming it and saving them. Peter, however, was impatient in his fear and forgot the almighty strength of his Lord. In his doubt, he risked drowning in a turbulent sea rather than keeping faith in Christ's promises.

Peter walked on the water as Christ did, sinking only when fear overtook him. Peter wasn't entirely faithless, or he might have leaped from the boat in desperation, risking his life in the water. Instead, he saw safety in Christ and asked to approach Him. His actions were prompted by fear, but tempered by faith. It was weak and imperfect faith, but it was true. Peter understood that Christ would save him but seemed to be unable to believe it when he took his eyes off Him. Christ not only saved Peter, but He also calmed the storm. These actions were critical in instructing His disciples because they, once again, proved the power and importance of keeping true faith.

We all struggle with doubt and shaken faith from time to time because we are all imperfect, fearful and lost in a chaotic world. We all make mistakes; it's what makes us human. A mistake, however, does not negate our faith. It demands that we fix that mistake and learn from its consequences. Only when we continue to trust in the Lord and seek to improve ourselves spiritually do we commit ourselves to having real faith.

Exposing Yourself to Faith

When you climb among the mountains, you are often exposed to demanding terrain and weather. Being so high up, you must rely on your skill and fortitude to bring you back down safely. The experience fills your senses: the feel of the rock, the smell of the earth, and the taste of the clean, crisp air. You are at the mercy of nature. It can make a person feel very small and insignificant, not to mention terrified. Some peaks have **ledge systems** that host severe **drop-offs**. Imagine sliding along a rocky ledge when only a few steps away is a fall of more than a thousand feet. Feeling queasy? I know I am when I see how easy it would be to plummet downward. You start asking yourself, what if I'm not strong enough? What if I slip? What if I start to panic? Am I already panicking? You're exposed to all the elements on that ledge, and you have to trust in your own fortitude to pass along it safely. Who wouldn't be terrified?

We have all felt some measure of this doubt, even if not in such a death-defying way. Any time we stand up in front of an audience, play a sport or even take a test, our bodies can be overrun with anxiety. You doubt your ability to perform, let alone perform well. We all have ledges we balance along with individual dangers and consequences should we stumble. But if we practice and commit ourselves to the challenge, do we not improve? When we begin to succeed at our given task, our confidence builds and strengthens our trust in our own abilities. It's the same with faith. The harder you try to reinforce your faith, the more you will see the power of God at work. The clearer your vision, the greater your trust will be in the Lord.

Derrick Coleman is a fullback with the 2014 Superbowl champions, the Seattle Seahawks. He is also the first deaf offensive player in NFL history. He has worn hearing aids from the age of 3, which often makes playing football difficult because he cannot hear the calls made by coaches and teammates. On top of that, his hearing aids often fall out during games and practices. Despite his handicap, he received a full scholarship to UCLA, only to remain undrafted after graduation. For a time, he bounced around on practice squads until 2012, when the Seahawks added him to their starting team. Now he has a championship ring.

In a Duracell commercial, Coleman talked about all of the times he was told to quit because he would never make it as a legally deaf player. He said, "They told me that it could never be done, but I've been deaf since 3, so I didn't listen." I love this line. He did not say, "I *couldn't* listen," but "I *didn't* listen." He made a choice to persevere and ignore the naysayers. Despite the many struggles Coleman faced through his young life, he came out stronger.

We all struggle with faith at times because there's no easy path through life. When we think we have taken a step forward, we get pulled two steps back. When we're finally sure of our footing, something inevitably comes along that makes us falter. Peter, while walking on the water toward Christ, became suddenly afraid of the storm and lost his footing. Instead of marveling at the miracle before him, he was engulfed by the chaos; he was weighed down with fear and doubt until he literally began to sink. Peter had enough faith to get out of the boat, but not enough to take those few extra steps to Christ's saving embrace. Experience taught Peter that man cannot walk on water and that nothing is stronger than nature's wrath; thus, he faltered. It is difficult to balance what we *know* with what we *believe*, but we must always remember that in Christ all things are possible (Philippians 4:13).

How easy would it be for you to name three pressures you face in a given day? Think of pressures you face at school or at home. Perhaps at a part-time job or extracurricular activity. The reality is we're bombarded with these external issues throughout our lives; they never go away, but dealing with them does become easier. You will grow stronger, smarter and better equipped to stare them down. Right now you are only beginning to climb your mountain, to strengthen your faith and skills so that you can take on whatever lies ahead. Jesus does not expect us to always take a step in faith and never fall back again. He does not ask us to be perfect. He asks us to be courageous enough to take that step forward even when the path appears narrow and riddled with obstacles. No matter how slow our progress, it's still progress.

Take Hold of His Hand

The best days hiking a peak can also be the worst. You hike almost 20 miles, your feet are killing you, and your knees feel like rubber. Your whole body is screaming at you to just stop already. You begin to shake uncontrollably because your body has no energy left to maintain **core temperature**, and you begin to wonder why you put yourself through all of it. Then you reach the end of the path and look over the world from a height few have ever achieved. Words fail to describe the scene before you or the triumph you feel upon seeing it. No matter how many people came before, your victory is unique; no one will see it with your eyes or your personal experience. You were challenged and even questioned your own resolve, but in the end, you conquered your personal mountain, for which there can be no greater achievement.

Conquering a challenge produces maturity in faith. When the boat faltered in the storm, the disciples doubted. Peter did not have perfect faith. Was it not Peter, after all, who denied his Lord three times (Matthew 26:69-75)? The best thing about making mistakes is that it can motivate us to try harder the next time. After he stumbled on the water, Peter was still saved by Christ. Despite his doubt, he was not forsaken but given another lesson and the chance to strengthen his faith. After denying Jesus three times, Peter did not forsake his faith but took up the role of evangelist after Christ's death. Along with Paul, he promoted the establishment of Christ's church (Acts 1:15) and, according to church tradition, died a martyr's death in defense of his beliefs (John 21:18-19). When Peter faltered, the challenge to rise up fortified his faith in Christ.

We are fortunate to live when we do because we are free to believe. We need not die for Christ, but dedicate our hearts to spreading His glory. When Christ plucked Peter from the water, He asked, "O you of little faith, why did you doubt?" Christ is ever merciful. He does not expect miracles from us any more than He did from His disciples. We are asked only to strengthen our faith so that it might not be overcome by doubt; we are asked to trust in the Lord to be beside us, guiding us forward to safety. If Peter's faith had been steadier, he would have walked on the water beside Christ. Instead, he faltered and continued to hesitate until Christ's resurrection, when he repented for his doubt (John 21:15-17).

There was no punishment for Peter's weakness. Christ saved him and calmed the storm, bolstering His disciples' faith even though Peter stumbled: "And when they got into the boat, the wind ceased. And those in the boat worshiped him, saying, 'Truly you are the Son of God'" (Matthew 14:32-33). The disciples were tested and given proof of Christ's divinity. I cannot imagine they ever forgot that moment when their mentor stood on suddenly calm waters, asking why they had doubted Him. It is not something anyone would likely forget.

Believe it or not, we all experience these moments of revelation, even if less miraculous. Was it that time you scored the winning goal? Perhaps the time when you traveled abroad? It could have been something less noticeable, like passing a class you never thought you would understand, or getting your first job or driver's license. It does not need to be a groundbreaking event to change you for the better.

One Step at a Time

While climbing mountains, I have often come across someone who has taken on the challenge of climbing a peak too advanced for his or her level of experience. Although it is important to step forward and to push yourself back to your feet after you have fallen, you should not risk your life. These hikers, who do not have the experience or skill appropriate for tackling more dangerous peaks, are usually over-confident and trust in false skills.

Once I was climbing a peak with a **couloir** (a large **crevasse** between two steep **gradients**). During the winter, these couloirs fill with snow and ice, which remain on the mountain for the majority of the summer. Two hikers were ahead of my group, attempting to **scale** up this couloir, which was nothing more than a sheet of ice. There was no room for error in this environment; you had to be sure of your equipment, as well as of yourself, and remain aware of the weather and terrain to avoid an accident. These two hikers were moving steadily along when one, who was only a little way up the gap, began to panic. Overwhelmed by the situation, he returned to a point of comfort further down the slope.

What would have happened if he had kept going? For one, he could have succeeded in conquering his fear and learned more about climbing in such conditions. On the other hand, he could have fallen or suffered an accident due to his lack of skill. Retreat in this instance is acceptable so long as it does not result in a weakened spirit. If he continues to climb and practice, this man will build confidence in his skills and trust in his abilities. Although he moved back one step, he can still go forward two if he is committed to improving himself. When he does choose to tackle that peak again, he will find it waiting for him, and when he finally reaches the summit, the rush of triumph will be all the more wondrous. This is what Christ taught His disciples.

Building your faith is no different than studying for school or practicing for a game: it takes dedication, commitment and the belief that you *can* achieve something greater. Often this means leaving behind the familiar and allowing yourself to be buffeted by the chaotic storms of life. To accomplish this, we need faith in Christ but also in ourselves. We need to trust what we have learned and hold fast to those principles. However, we must also ask for help when we need it. Christ might not reach out a physical hand to you as He did to Peter, but He encourages us through the love shown to us by our family and friends, urging us to trust that everything will be all right in the end. We must simply remember that when we are once again ready to take those steps forward, God will be waiting, and our triumph will be all the more extraordinary.

Discussion Questions

1. In Matthew 14:30, why did Peter begin to sink after he left the boat? Do you think this experience made his faith stronger?

2. What challenges do you think have made you stronger as a person?

3. How does Derrick Coleman's resilience to adversity relate to strengthened faith? How can these types of stories motivate you to overcome various challenges in your own life?

4. What are some practical ways in which you can learn to trust God more in your life?

CLIMBING 101

Acclimation

People often become sick when hiking and climbing mountains. The most typical problem is altitude sickness. The higher you go, the less oxygen there is to breathe, which causes the blood to thicken and causes headaches, nausea, and, ultimately, blackouts. Elevation influences everyone differently. You could be a great athlete at sea level but barely able to walk when at 12,000 feet. Some people will struggle with altitude, while others, like my nephews from Tennessee, can come from sea level and keep up with teens from Colorado. The best way to overcome altitude sickness is to allow your body to acclimate. This just means that you spend time at higher altitudes, allowing your body and mind to adapt to new temperatures and elevations. It also helps to take an aspirin, which thins the blood, and to drink plenty of water.

Acclimation is also a Christian principle. We are exposed to many different things during our lives, and we must adapt to them if we want to succeed. This is not a new concept. Even Paul wrote to the Romans, "Do not be conformed to this world, but be transformed by the renewal of your mind, that by testing you may discern what is the will of God, what is good and acceptable and perfect" (Romans 12:2). Your body and mind will adapt to whatever choices you make; it is up to you to make the right ones.

4

Faith or Habit
Matthew 15:1-20

Imagine you are hiking up a mountain. It's not your first time, but for whatever reason, you take a wrong step and are clinging to the rock with the certain knowledge that you cannot regain your footing. Your friend is secure above and lowers a rope for you to grab onto; it's the only way you are going to get off this rock face safely, but you hesitate. You have never used a rope to climb before, though you keep one with you for emergencies. You pride yourself on tackling every mountain "bare-handed" because it is how you have always done it and how you intend to carry on. No one else would think less of you for taking your friend's rope, not when it is a matter of life and death. Still, you hesitate because you would think less of yourself. Habit has become so ingrained in your brain that you actually think about rejecting the rope.

That is an extreme example, I admit, but it is valid. We all have habits or traditions in our lives that become so second-nature we no longer think about them. When these routines are broken, we often feel confused, frustrated or even lost. We are creatures of habit who crave order and routine. But when does habit overcome belief? Do you attend church at the same time every week because that is what you have always done? Do you offer up prayers out of routine? Are these things habit, or are they a sign of your commitment to the Lord? When do we stop actively seeking Christ and simply slip into routine?

More than once I have heard young adults say they attend church because it is expected of them. They continue to attend because they have always gone to church. This is passive faith; they worship out of habit, not because they seek salvation. Jesus, however, does not want you to sit idly; He wants you to embrace Him as He has embraced you. He does not want you to fear changing routine or breaking habits if that leads to a life lived for Him. A church is guilty of sin when, instead of holding every member accountable and challenging the congregation in Christ, it accepts passive attendance and passive faith. We want to believe weekly attendance in church proves we are good Christians, but it does not. True faith is born of a commitment to love Christ as He loves us; faith demands an active struggle for growth in the Lord, where the only expectation is trust in His pure goodness.

Matthew 15:1-20

1 Then Pharisees and scribes came to Jesus from Jerusalem and said,

2 "Why do your disciples break the tradition of the elders? For they do not wash their hands when they eat."

3 He answered them, "And why do you break the commandment of God for the sake of your tradition?

4 "For God commanded, 'Honor your father and your mother,' and, 'Whoever reviles father or mother must surely die.'

5 "But you say, 'If anyone tells his father or his mother, "What you would have gained from me is given to God,"

6 " 'he need not honor his father.' So for the sake of your tradition you have made void the word of God.

7 "You hypocrites! Well did Isaiah prophesy of you, when he said:

8 " 'This people honors me with their lips, but their heart is far from me;

9 'in vain do they worship me, teaching as doctrines the commandments of men.'"

10 And he called the people to him and said to them, "Hear and understand:

11 "it is not what goes into the mouth that defiles a person, but what comes out of the mouth; this defiles a person."

12 Then the disciples came and said to him, "Do you know that the Pharisees were offended when they heard this saying?"

13 He answered, "Every plant that my heavenly Father has not planted will be rooted up.

14 "Let them alone; they are blind guides. And if the blind lead the blind, both will fall into a pit."

15 But Peter said to him, "Explain the parable to us."

16 And he said, "Are you also still without understanding?

17 "Do you not see that whatever goes into the mouth passes into the stomach and is expelled?

18 "But what comes out of the mouth proceeds from the heart, and this defiles a person.

19 "For out of the heart come evil thoughts, murder, adultery, sexual immorality, theft, false witness, slander.

20 "These are what defile a person. But to eat with unwashed hands does not defile anyone."

The Pharisees approached Christ about His breaking with Hebrew tradition (Matthew 15:1-2). The disciples, not fully understanding Christ's message, asked for clarification, and Jesus obliged: "Do you not see that whatever goes into the mouth passes into the stomach and is expelled? But what comes out of the mouth proceeds from the heart, and this defiles a person" (vv. 17-18). Christ was attempting to educate His followers about the difference between the traditions of men and the commandments of God. What did it matter if their hands were clean when they ate? The food, dirtied or not, affected no one spiritually; it could not defile a person as murder or immorality could. The Pharisees compared a stomachache to damnation simply for the sake of tradition.

When the Pharisees demanded an explanation for the so-called flouting of Jewish tradition, Christ refused to give in to their authority. Instead, He demanded to know why they broke one of God's commandments (Matthew 15:3-9). Jewish tradition called for dedicated gifts, such as money or personal possessions, at the temple in God's name. In doing so, however, these people were depriving themselves of necessary supplies. Such gifts could not be taken back if, for example, a family member became ill or frail; the poor were pressed to offer such gifts instead of saving them for times of need. Christ called this tradition into question because it opposed the will of God (5:19-24). How could these men, self-proclaimed elders of their people, chastise Christ and His followers when they themselves broke not a law of man but one of God?

Habitual Traditions

Jesus was a revolutionary. He questioned routine and sought out truth, despite the long-established traditions of His people. Unlike many of His time, Jesus was not satisfied to follow routine or adhere to something simply because that was the way it had always been done. He was not content to rest among the idle flock, but chose to take up the shepherd's crook and lead His people down a new path of enlightenment. He wanted His followers to assess these preconceived notions of right and wrong and compare them to God's laws.

In America, people so often go to church expecting something like hotel service. They presume that people will be overly courteous, always aiming to please and willing to bend over backward to accommodate their every need. This isn't what church is. If you're looking for empty pampering, go to a hotel or spa. If you want to honor the Lord, seek salvation and share His love with the world, then go to church. Expectation, habit and routine all create a false sense of reality. You begin to take things for granted when they are always there. For example, going to college and having to do your own laundry for the first time is a shock, especially after years of having someone else do it for you – this I know from experience. Suddenly you have to figure out how to take care of menial tasks because you never needed to learn them before.

High Expectations

More than once, I have heard of members leaving a church because of a small, petty issue. One such example involved a person who left because another member was rude. I'm not condoning rude behavior, but it still seems a silly reason for leaving the church. Perhaps that person had other reasons, but the straw that broke the camel's back was a single instance of discourtesy. Some people have high demands for the church but low expectations for their personal commitment to service. We not only hurt ourselves with such expectations but also everyone around us.

Once I visited a young man in the hospital who overdosed on heroin. Because he was unconscious, my presence was more of a comfort for his mother and grandmother. A friend of the patient was also there. The family invited this young man to join us in prayer and also to come to worship services. We offered him support and comfort because he was suffering; the patient had little to no brain activity, and the doctor feared he would not recover. We did not want the other young man left alone with his pain. He declined our offer because a previous church experience had left him jaded. I don't know what he was told, but his impression was that he was a hopeless case and his sins could never be forgiven.

Each of us has had a bad experience that makes us avoid certain people or places. It's easier to harbor a grudge than to try again. When this man explained his reluctance to attend services, I replied: "You too? I've been mistreated by many church-goers myself." I wanted him to know he was not alone; we all struggle from time to time. Just because we attend church does not mean we are perfect, and we should not allow a few negative experiences with fallible people to stop us from worshiping the Lord and living for Him.

You are going to be mistreated from time to time. There will always be that rude or hypocritical person who thinks he or she is right with the Lord and can treat you as an inferior. You need to remember, in such instances, that you are not there for those people; you are not in church because it is expected. You are there for Christ. He will see your faith grow when you turn the other cheek to these weak believers, and He will smile upon you.

Invigorated Faith

We all have traditions. Some are passed down from generation to generation and unique to your family. Others are national, such as holidays and observances that commemorate moments of our collective past. Then there are our spiritual traditions. Each Sunday we attend services to honor Christ's glory and the gift of salvation He bestowed upon us. When you sit there, listening to the same stories, repeating the same phrases, going through the same motions, do you ever think, "Why am I here? What is this all about?" I would not be surprised if you do, because I have done it too. We so easily forget the purpose behind these traditions when they become routine.

Matthew 15 is an attempt to shake the reader awake and scatter the daydreams from his or her eyes. Christ aggressively defended His actions to the Pharisees, condemning them in the same breath for their own sins. He does not want idle listeners but motivators of the faith and disciples who actively seek spiritual improvement. Look at the many examples of the faithful in the New Testament: the sick and infirm, the downtrodden and ridiculed, the outcast and lost. These are the ones Christ sought, the ones He helped. The people who struggled yet kept the faith were blessed, all while His followers struggled to understand what He tried to teach.

After Jesus replied to the Pharisees' demand for explanation in Matthew 15:3-9, His disciples needed further clarification: "Then the disciples came and said to him, 'Do you know that the Pharisees were offended when they heard this saying?'" (v. 12). I marvel at Christ's patience and His ability to repeat these lessons over and over again. He called out the elders of the Jewish people for corruption and greed, calling them hypocrites of God's laws. The disciples, however, feared the Pharisees' reaction. They feared the possible repercussions they might suffer for Christ's bold words.

Immediately after His second explanation, a Canaanite woman approached Jesus. She was not of the faith, but she saw Christ's glory and knew He alone could save her daughter from the torment of a demon. At first, Jesus ignored her (Matthew 15:22-23). Then He explained He came to preach the gospel to the Jews, not the heathens, adding: "It is not right to take the children's bread and throw it to the dogs" (v. 26). These words compared her state to that of a lowly dog. Did she become enraged and spurn Him with vile words? Did she storm off angrily and curse Him? No. She replied, "Yes, Lord, yet even the dogs eat the crumbs that fall from their masters' table" (v. 27). This woman humbled herself at His feet because she saw His glory where others could not. She was willing to take whatever Christ offered, aware of her position as a heathen and His purpose among the Jews.

The Canaanite woman was the exact opposite of the Pharisees. She was not blinded by tradition or custom as were the disciples and Jews. Instead, her status as an outsider allowed her to see straight to the truth of Christ's divinity. He tested the woman with His words, only to bless her with her daughter's renewed health when the woman remained humble and true (Matthew 15:28). The Pharisees and the disciples questioned Jesus, seeking constant explanation for what He did and said. They were burdened with habit and blinded by tradition.

Have you ever sat in a class and had your mind wander? Your eyes might start to get heavy, your body twitchy; you might start to doodle on your notes or text a friend. I've done it. I think everyone has. Sitting still for a long period of time and trying to keep your brain active is exhausting. Listening to a sermon is not much different. Habit is boring. Routine is exhausting. We need activity to keep us moving and new ideas to stimulate mental growth. This is what Christ attempted to teach His followers; passive faith is unacceptable. We need to remember *why* we sit in church and *why* we listen to sermons. Only then will we break free of habit and actively live in the Lord and be blessed in His sight.

Discussion Questions

1. Is your faith something you do out of habit or obedience? How can you tell the difference?

2. How can you overcome developing a passive faith, which blindly follows traditions instead of truth?

3. In Matthew 15:1-2, what did Jesus refuse to do that the Pharisees and scribes considered proof of true faith? Is there a time when you should stand against the traditions of men? How do you correctly discern when these times occur?

4. We all have expectations of our church and the people therein. What are some of your expectations? Have you ever witnessed demands by other people that you found wrong?

5. In the Bible, many men and women were willing to suffer and be mistreated rather than relinquish their faith. What was their motivation?

CLIMBING 101

Lifelines

What I do is considered safe when compared to some of the more extreme mountaineering done around the world. When I hike, I always have an experienced partner; we use ropes when necessary and follow established routes previously taken by other trained hikers. There are those, however, who undertake "free soloing." This is a form of free climbing where climbers hike alone and don't use ropes, harnesses or other protective gear while ascending; they rely solely on their climbing abilities. These climbers go beyond safe heights where a fall most certainly means serious injury or death. This style of climbing has produced a famous expression: "There are bold climbers and old climbers, but there are no old, bold climbers."

We might think that free soloing is crazy, but we can act just as crazy with our own morality. Sometimes Christians practice free soloing by attending events that place them in the center of temptation. Someone who struggles with drinking has no business going to a bar, just like a Christian would be foolish to attend parties where numerous sinful activities are taking place. Never forget, however, that these death-defying actions are choices; there are always ropes and helping hands available if you ask for them.

5

Gear of Faith

Ephesians 6:10-17

Anyone who has ever taken up a new hobby understands that having the right equipment is a necessity. You can hardly play football without a football or a video game without the right controller. What about quality? If you were not experienced in a sport or activity, would you buy the more expensive gear or the cheaper version, just in case you decided to quit sooner rather than later? I like to play it safe and start small; I won't buy those golf clubs for $500 if I can get a used set at a thrift store for $25. After all, why would I invest in something I am not sure I will even like? If I find out this new activity is not for me, then I can walk away without having wasted a lot of money. If I decide I like it, then I commit to it, regardless of time and cash consumption.

I went through this process when I started mountain climbing. I tackled my first few fourteeners wearing a $30 pair of boots I bought at a thrift shop. The following year, I admitted I needed something better and made a few $100 purchases. By the third year, however, I easily dropped $200 on new boots alone! This increase in spending was not only because I loved climbing but also because I wanted my gear to last and keep me safe. The original pair of cheap, thrift-shop boots fell apart quickly from the rigorous terrain. The traction was never very good, and by the end, they had no grip whatsoever. Worse yet, they gave me painful blisters. So I upgraded. I spent time researching what I would need and committed to buying a decent pair of boots. When you are in a life or death situation, you need to trust in your gear, which means you need to ensure it is of the best quality.

Ephesians 6:10-17

10 Finally, be strong in the Lord and in the strength of his might.

11 Put on the whole armor of God, that you may be able to stand against the schemes of the devil.

12 For we do not wrestle against flesh and blood, but against the rulers, against the authorities, against the cosmic powers over this present darkness, against the spiritual forces of evil in the heavenly places.

13 Therefore take up the whole armor of God, that you may be able to withstand in the evil day, and having done all, to stand firm.

14 Stand therefore, having fastened on the belt of truth, and having put on the breastplate of righteousness,

15 and, as shoes for your feet, having put on the readiness given by the gospel of peace.

16 In all circumstances take up the shield of faith, with which you can extinguish all the flaming darts of the evil one;

17 and take the helmet of salvation, and the sword of the Spirit, which is the word of God,

In Ephesians 6, Paul described the weapons of the Lord, the gear for a life of faith. This gear is useless, however, if we hide within the comforts of the church. If we never attempt to share our faith, go on a mission trip or serve others, we don't need good gear; we just need a pew to sit on. God wants the armor to be used to defend us against wickedness and enable us to fight against Satan's schemes.

In Ephesians 6:10-13, Paul instructed us to stand before God and against Satan wearing the armor of your faith. Wear each and every piece, for only when the armor is whole will you be best protected from the devil. If you omit one element – truth, righteousness, faith – then you are vulnerable. Walk along the path of the gospel and wield the Word as your sword; with these things you will find safety and strength.

You might wonder at Paul's excessive use of military terminology when Christ preached passive resistance and brotherly love. Passivity, however, does not exclude fighting; rather, it suggests a different form of attack. Christ asked us to be warriors by committing ourselves to the faith and its defense. Armed with knowledge and belief, we are stronger against the hidden war for our souls. If we stay alert and hone our skills, we shall remain protected against Satan and his forces. Only in a moment of weakness, idleness or indifference will our armor fail.

Armor for the Soul

It's easy to recite the words of Christ and Paul but difficult to live by them. How do we know when the armor is securely fastened or that we are properly armed against the works of evil in the world? We can prepare for inclement weather by checking the reports; we can be confident in our sports apparel because we can inspect it. The armor of God, however, is invisible and acquired only through faith. We cannot see it. We cannot test it. But we can be certain it will survive any and all battles against wickedness and sin.

Building your personal, spiritual armor is like playing a video game. Think about role-playing video games such as *World of Warcraft*. This game allows you to choose a character and experience fantastical adventures with other players around the world. The only way to succeed within the game is to acquire swords, shields and various other items, which allow you to improve your avatar. Unless you develop your character's skills and equip him or her with better weapons, you have no way to be successful. Similarly, we go to school to arm ourselves with knowledge so we can succeed in adult life; athletes practice so they can be recruited by better teams. These activities are, essentially, the same in that they require focus, commitment and the desire for self-improvement.

However, we are not reinforcing our "armor" for recognition

or fame; we are not playing a game, but the ultimate battle of good versus evil. To be successful, we must equip ourselves appropriately. That means reinforcing our spiritual armor by having the focus, commitment and desire to go to church, read the Bible and engage in community service so we can strengthen our spirits. People spend countless hours playing online games even though these are only virtual simulations. Imagine how strong their Christian character would be if they dedicated the same amount of time to improving their spirits.

Early last spring, a friend of mine was going to climb Little Bear Peak. During this time of year, a good amount of snow is usually still on the mountains, which means you need specific equipment to help you climb. We bought **crampons**, which are metal spikes that attach to your boots in order to provide traction when hiking in snowy or icy conditions. I went to a sports store with high-quality merchandise. My friend, however, ordered a set of used crampons online. When his order arrived, he discovered they were more than 40 years old with worn leather straps; they would not stay on his feet no matter how tightly he thought they were tied. Frustrated, he opted for **microspikes** over the aged crampons.

I think we can agree that the old crampons would have given him no traction on the mountain, but his decision to get microspikes was no better. They never provided the right amount of grip or security during the climb, forcing him to go slower and stumble along. Had he educated himself on the conditions and what was needed to climb the peak safely, he would have been better equipped and **ascended** more smoothly and with greater confidence. Mistakes happen; we will never get it right all the time. But if we improve ourselves and commit to understanding what is needed in a given situation, we are more likely to triumph.

If you go on a hike, you will need a checklist of important equipment: sleeping bags to keep warm, food to eat, water to drink and gear to climb safely. Paul left us the ultimate list for our journey along the upward climb through life. Not only will we be confronted by Satan, but also by social pressure, economic hardship and the everyday trials of life. But we need to remember we are not alone in our struggle. God is with us always, and those who came before us left a guide to support us in troubled times. God also accounted for every possible tactic Satan might employ in tripping us up and turning our good intentions toward sin.

Your Only Weapon

Arming ourselves, however, is only half the battle. Paul told us to take up the sword of the Spirit, which is the Word of God. He did not mean that we should spout doctrine but that we should abide by God's laws and live each day according to His mandates. Words are useless if we don't put them into action. We cannot promote the path of Christ if we cannot lead by example. A time will come when you hear false doctrine because the pride of men easily blinds them to truth. They will read the Word of God incorrectly and attempt to sway others, but if you have faith and trust in the Lord, you will not succumb. You will be armed with the gear of the righteous and protected against the hypocrites and liars. Maintain this equipment, and Satan will be unable to attack; improve upon it, and you will guide others by example.

I once heard that Tiger Woods can tell you exactly what ingredients are used in a given golf ball. All he needs to do is hit the ball off a tee, and he knows its material. Woods uses only the best balls because the quality makes a difference in his game. If I play a round of golf, the quality of the ball does not matter, because I still do not have the skills to hit it properly. A pro athlete wants the best because he or she knows how to use it. Similarly, the sword of the Spirit is effective only in the hands of the truly righteous – those who live for the Lord and obey His Word.

Stand Firm

This is all well and good, but how do we stand firm? How do we apply what Paul commanded to our daily lives? We have been told what we need to keep our souls intact but not how to acquire shields, swords and helmets. These are items so far removed from our modern mentality that they are difficult to take seriously, even if we understand they are simply metaphors. Warfare today is always at a distance for Americans; it happens somewhere else and seems far removed from our lives. The battle for our souls, however, is ever-present, and we must be prepared to stand against it. Just as you would dress for a rainstorm or blizzard, you must also dress yourself for the constant, though subtle, fight against evil. This begins with trusting the Lord to provide for you, care for you and protect you from harm. God is always watching over you and asks only that you commit your hearts to His glory.

As in a real battle, we must seek tactical success; we must search for the higher ground of morality and maintain it at all costs against Satan's army. If we strengthen our faith and live each day in the Lord, then we assist Him in building an army of righteousness.

In 1 Peter 5:8-10, Peter taught that we must be true to ourselves. Self-confidence is the first step to removing weakness from ourselves and, therefore, to strengthening our souls against Satan and his schemes. Peter also emphasized the amplified power of a united community living for the Lord. Together, we can stand against the army of darkness and its many cunning plots, reserving our place at the right hand of God.

Satan works through trickery, falsehood and cunning. Like a bully, he preys on our weaknesses, exposing them until we falter along God's path. He spouts lies, hiding behind them as a bully hides behind strength, size or anger. Paul told his audience to wear the belt of truth – that is, the knowledge of the Lord and the promises given through His Son. If we remember all Christ taught – to love one another, forgive and live for God – then Satan's manipulative words should not turn us down the path of darkness.

When you study for a test, you're building your confidence in the material so that you can succeed in showing your understanding of the subject. Yet sometimes we study hard for something only to sit down and panic because everything in our minds goes blank as we begin to second-guess what we know. This is what Satan does to our faith. He introduces doubt because he wants us to second-guess what we know to be true so that he can turn our eyes from the Lord. If you let Satan control and influence your mind, he will win the battle for your soul. Through his ill advice and your lack of belief, he will obstruct your path to Christ by pulling you into sin. Doubt is easily removed by equipping yourselves as Paul recommended. Shod your feet in the gospel of peace so that you can walk with the truth given by Jesus to His disciples. Bear always the shield of faith, which is proof of your belief in the Almighty. Keep about you the belt of truth, the breastplate of righteousness, the helmet of salvation; with these things you will be protected against Satan's ploys and delivered safely to the Lord, stronger and more blessed than ever before.

Discussion Questions

1. What is the importance of having the right gear? Does it make a difference?

2. In Ephesians 6:14-17, Paul mentioned many pieces of armor and battle gear. What are they, and why are they important? For what battle was Paul preparing his readers?

3. How do we strengthen our faith through battle while not allowing it to be defeated in battle?

4. What are some strategies to sharpen the sword of the Spirit?

5. Can you be successful in the battle against Satan with only some of the gear Paul described? Why, or why not?

CLIMBING 101

Brands

Mountain climbers are pretty particular about their equipment. For instance, most true mountaineers refuse to use the brand The North Face, even though it extremely popular. The North Face presents itself as an outdoor company, but for climbers in Colorado it is mostly associated with suburbanites who have never been near a mountain, let alone climbed one. Most climbers I have met prefer the brand Mountain Hardwear, which was founded in 1993 by a small group of avid outdoorsmen and women committed to advancing technology and equipment for true mountaineers. The company sponsors many climbers, like Ed Viesturs, who was the first American to climb all 14 eight-thousanders in the Himalayan and Karakoram ranges in Asia. They also sponsor Erik Weihenmayer, the only blind person to summit Mount Everest. The experiences of these climbers provided firsthand research for Mountain Hardwear so the company could perfect its gear and equipment

It is not the brand, however, that makes the climber. The North Face and Mountain Hardwear merely supply equipment that can assist the **alpinist**, mountaineer or even the most casual enthusiast with the ability to achieve new heights. In the same way, it is not the label "Christian" that makes us true followers of Christ, but how we use the tools He provided us with to live according to His Word.

6

Path to Joy
Luke 18:35-43

Everyone has an opinion on the weather. Take snow, for instance. Some people love it and cannot wait for the first flakes to fall. These are the friends who post pictures of snow on Facebook with a dozen exclamation points. They love the appearance of fresh snow on the ground, no matter how much or how little. For all the reasons someone loves snow, others hate it. Driving in icy or slushy conditions is the worst; it slows down the commute and causes accidents, not to mention the high heating bills and the damages caused by freezing temperatures. I have known people to move to different parts of the country just to avoid another snowy winter. During a hike, people have different opinions on snow. Some love hiking in snow while others complain the entire time about the white, cold substance. It is, however, a matter of individual opinion: you hate it, or you love it; you complain about it, or you enjoy it.

The varied opinions on snow aren't that different from the attitudes toward faith. There are those who accept it as a blessing, but some are apathetic or actually hate the very idea of it. Militant atheists refer to faith as a "crutch" that limits the believer from living in the here and now. They associate believing in God to believing in a fairy tale and mark it as a waste of time. Faith to such

63

people is pointless because it offers no instantaneous, measurable results; they are unable to see beyond the physical and temporal to something greater. People who have faith and believe in this greater something know that it's the anchor of reality. Faith sustains life and provides hope for a better tomorrow. It compels us to live by a moral code and fills us with joy. At times it is difficult to navigate through doubt and fear just as it is difficult to see our way through a wintry storm. In the end, however, we always return to the comforting and loving embrace of the Lord, who is the greatest haven in the storms of life.

Luke 18:35-43

35 As he drew near to Jericho, a blind man was sitting by the roadside begging.

36 And hearing a crowd going by, he inquired what this meant.

37 They told him, "Jesus of Nazareth is passing by."

38 And he cried out, "Jesus, Son of David, have mercy on me!"

39 And those who were in front rebuked him, telling him to be silent. But he cried out all the more, "Son of David, have mercy on me!"

40 And Jesus stopped and commanded him to be brought to him. And when he came near, he asked him,

41 "What do you want me to do for you?" He said, "Lord, let me recover my sight."

42 And Jesus said to him, "Recover your sight; your faith has made you well."

43 And immediately he recovered his sight and followed him, glorifying God. And all the people, when they saw it, gave praise to God.

The journey of faith often begins with a sense of need. We need comfort and understanding; we need to believe we belong to something greater; we need to believe we are not alone in a large, chaotic world. Some view such admissions as signs of weakness and see faith itself as the crutch people use to hobble through life. Confident unbelievers see no purpose in asking for help because they think they are self-sufficient. When we are young, we think nothing of seeking assistance, but as we age, we shy from admitting when we cannot act alone. In our minds, independence is tied so tightly with maturity that the loss of one implies the loss of the other. Unbelievers worship this independence without looking outside themselves. On the other hand, believers open their hearts with humility. You realize you are one person in a large world and sometimes you need a helping hand.

Luke 18 relates a story of a man who ignored pride and opened his heart to Christ. Mentioned by name in Mark 10:46, Bartimaeus, a blind beggar, was sitting along the road leading into Jericho when Christ passed by. The beggar rose to his feet and cried out to gain Christ's attention. Even after the crowd shushed him, Bartimaeus was not ashamed of his faith and cried out with even greater fervor. His story teaches the rewards we receive when we worship without shame.

Unashamed Faith

Some time ago, a girls youth group I am familiar with had a sleepover where they decided to watch the movie *Mean Girls*. It's about a group of high school girls who believe they are better than everyone else and bully their classmates into doing what they want. The movie contains sex, drinking, partying, betrayal, backstabbing, gossiping, lying and immodesty – not exactly a good movie for the impressionable minds of 11- and 12-year-old girls. So one of the girls suggested a different movie with less immorality.

Ironically, the rest of the girls started making fun of her. They teased and mocked the girl until they got their way. Maybe they were embarrassed for wanting to watch such a perverse movie. Maybe they realized it was inappropriate but didn't want to admit they were wrong. Instead of accepting the one girl's idea, they shamed her into staying silent and watched the movie anyway. The girl was so afraid of standing alone or losing her friends that she kept quiet, despite her better judgment.

Unlike the girl, Bartimaeus unashamedly separated himself from the group and professed his belief in Christ: "And he cried out, 'Jesus, Son of David, have mercy on me!' And those who were in front rebuked him, telling him to be silent. But he cried out all the more, 'Son of David, have mercy on me!'" (Luke 18:38-39). Risking ostracism and mockery, Bartimaeus had the strength to speak up when the crowd told him not to. It is difficult to match this fearlessness when dealing with the social chaos of high school or college, but only because we all forget what matters most. Our years as teens are brief, mere moments in our long lives. Our time in heaven, however, will be eternal.

Walking Blind

Bartimaeus' need deafened him to the rebukes of the crowd and, fueled by faith, drove him toward Christ. Perhaps this absence of genuine need restricts the growth of strong faith in America today. After all, what causes us to seek Christ if we do not need Him? If you are satisfied and content with your life, then you have little to no reason to seek aid from an external source. When you are sad, lonely or simply in need of comfort, you look to something else as a cure. A strong faith continues through times of contentment, when you have no great need, and remembers to give thanks for everything you have.

The people in Luke's story had become complacent in their faith. They celebrated Jesus, but it was not until the blind man's sight was restored that they truly *saw* His glory. They were metaphorically blind to the power of true faith; they were passive believers who were never challenged to strengthen their relationship with the Lord. They attempted to silence Bartimaeus, but why? Were they embarrassed or ashamed of his actions? Or was it something else? In the story, they attempted to bully him into silence because their faith was weak, just as a school bully attacks what he or she does not understand. Yet nothing ever shook Bartimaeus' belief in the power of Jesus. He risked further social isolation because, in the end, it would not matter. His need narrowed his focus, eliminating the inconsequential while amplifying his faith.

A few years ago, a friend and I were hiking Missouri Mountain.

Because it was early in the hiking season, there was still some snow left, but most of it was melting and raising the creek water to a really high level. Walking through a mountain creek that early in the year is no picnic; your feet feel like they are burning in the cold water, and if that is not enough, you feel like your very blood has turned to ice. Needless to say, we were hoping for a **snow bridge** over the creek. I even told my friend that I was praying for one as we came down the mountain.

As we descended, we strayed a little from the trail only to find a perfect snow bridge across the very creek we feared having to cross. I am not exaggerating when I say no other snow was around; everything had melted except for this one spot. Like any other snow bridge, it had formed over the creek, allowing the water to run smoothly under it. Relieved, we approached it, but I couldn't make myself cross. I was so afraid it wouldn't hold, and I would still end up in the freezing cold water. The next moment, my friend passed me, walking over the bridge to arrive safely on the other side. When I asked what he was doing, he replied: "You prayed for it. Let's have the faith to cross it." Neither of us ended up in the creek, I am happy to say, but it took faith and trust to walk over it.

It takes real trust and more than a little courage to continue to move forward in faith when the whole world seems against you. Sometimes, you yourself are the one who stands in your way, as I did at the snow bridge. I had doubts about its stability and feared what would happen if it gave way, but my friend did not. And even the smallest demonstration of real faith bears weight. If you choose not to attend a party or watch a movie because it's morally questionable, you will experience a moment of strong, true faith. If someone at school offers you drugs, asks you to cheat or hurts someone else, will you remain silent? Will you join in so that they don't turn on you? Or will you walk away and tell someone of authority what is happening? Each of these choices decides the path that will lead you forward through life, and the more popular way is often not the best way.

Matthew W. Morine

Walking in Faith

If Jesus is more important to you than the opinion of others, then you will remain strong in your faith. You will trust in God and continue to cry out to Him. The people telling you to keep quiet cannot save you, something Bartimaeus must have realized. What could the mob have done to help him? How many times had they passed him on the street without considering his suffering? And what harm could they have caused that he had not already suffered and conquered? Instead of cowering beneath their commands, Bartimaeus cried louder; his was a single voice, but it rang clear and true and brought Christ to his side.

Jesus commanded the crowd to bring the beggar forward and asked what He could do for the blind man. When Bartimaeus asked for his sight to be returned to him, Jesus replied: "Recover your sight; your faith has made you well" (Luke 18:42). His faith – his real, consistent faith – made him well. Imagine the scene. A blind beggar stood before the King, surrounded by fellow citizens of Jericho who had ignored his suffering until this moment. He could have requested anything of Christ, like wealth, a home, food, perhaps even revenge on those who refused to help him or tried to silence him. Instead, he asked for his sight, something we take for granted every day, something the people around him took for granted.

Bartimaeus trusted in Christ, believed in Him, and kept his faith strong despite the many challenges he faced in life. (Or was his faith strong because of the challenges he faced? (See James 1:2-3, 12.) When he recovered his sight, he became an example to all around him, reaffirming their weakened belief. The path of faith might seem solitary, but your actions affect those around you. If you stand up for yourself or someone else in need, others will take notice. Your courage to follow the righteous path assures the doubters or fearful that it's safe for them to act accordingly. If you decide not to go along with the crowd, you might be mocked or teased, but you're not alone. Others will agree with you; they only need to see your strength and conviction so they can stand with you. Sometimes we do not need to see a miracle to have faith; sometimes we just need the reassurance that we're not alone.

Jesus offered to help Bartimaeus because of his faith. Where before he believed in Christ without undeniable proof, now he could physically see God at work. Those who trust in God are never blind to His glory. Those who do not think faith is important or who doubt in God's benevolence are unable to see His presence in every facet of their lives. They live in darkness, without knowing the joy of living for the Lord. They cannot understand our faith and often will attempt to bully us into agreeing with their opinions. They try to silence us and make us forsake our faith. There is, however, no greater joy in life than seeing the power of God at work. Those who cry out to God and allow His power into their lives find fulfillment, happiness and purpose. You come to the Lord in need, are then filled with His glory, and find your heart restored and your spirit strengthened.

Faith is the ray of light breaking through a gray, stormy sky. It beckons you out of darkness and into the sunshine, asking only that you have the courage to walk the path. We need to have the strength to do so, the strength to stand for what we believe in rather than run from it. We need to open our eyes to new experiences because only when our eyes are truly open will we see the glory of God.

Discussion Questions

1. What is your opinion on faith? What brought you to Christ in the first place? More importantly, what has kept you there?

2. How did Bartimaeus react to being told to be quiet? Have you ever had to speak up for your faith? Was it awkward or empowering?

3. In Luke 18:42, Bartimaeus had bold faith. What did Jesus do for the beggar as a reward for that faith? What does bold faith look like to you?

4. In Luke 18:41, Jesus asked Bartimaeus a powerful question: "What do you want me to do for you?" If you had to answer that question right now, what would you say?

CLIMBING 101

Weather

During my hikes, I have walked through snow, against 60 mph winds, thunder and lightning storms, rain and perfectly blue skies, all within hours of each other. High-altitude hiking requires taking the weather seriously. For example, each year numerous people die in Colorado because of lightning strikes alone. There are certain measures you must take when a lightning storm catches you climbing. First of all, never lay flat on the ground; if the lightning strikes close to you, it can travel through your entire body and more than likely kill you. Instead, squat down and put your hands on your knees. This way, if you are hit, the charge will travel through your arms to your knees, avoiding your heart and other vital organs.

This is a worst-case scenario. It is better to be prepared for inclement weather rather than to try and survive it. Be aware of the forecast. Almost every afternoon in Colorado there will be thunder and lightning storms in the mountains. You need to give yourself enough time to follow the trailhead, reach the summit and descend safely below the tree line before the storm hits. If you remain aware of the many possible dangers on the road ahead, then you can prepare yourself to weather even the most terrible storms.

7

Safety Culture
Luke 19:1-10

During a climb on Wetterhorn Peak, I was coming down the mountain by myself and missed the turn for the trail. My friend was injured, so I was not thinking clearly and somehow ended up on the wrong side of the peak. I panicked. My friend was hurt, I was on the opposite side of the mountain, and I was completely lost and alone. What could I do? Should I try to retrace my steps back around to the path or stay off the path and hope to find a safe place to descend? Experience told me to go back. It is all too easy to come to a cliff and slip on loose rocks. The trails are there for a reason after all. When I calmed down, I turned back, climbed a class-three **chimney** (which is no easy feat), and found the path. I accepted my mistake, corrected it and helped my friend to safety.

Mistakes happen. You might come to an obstacle in your life and make the wrong decision. No one is perfect. What matters is how you deal with it. Do you ignore it and hope for the best? Or do you face it head-on and try to correct it to the best of your ability? Throwing up your hands and quitting solves nothing, though at times we want it to. What helps us through these times is our faith. Living for Christ means we are never truly alone or forgotten. When I was climbing Wetterhorn, desperate to find the trail, I was only physically alone. The Lord is always with us, even if we doubt it.

He wants us to triumph over these obstacles; He is rooting for us to win. But do not think He will remove the challenge. These speed bumps are necessary evils; from the decisions we make to how we handle the fallout, challenges and obstacles help define who we are.

These challenges also help us grow in Christ. Even if we wanted to be protected from the darkness of the world, there is no foolproof way to do so without stunting our own personal growth. If I could protect my children from the sins of modern society I would do so in a heartbeat. I want them to grow up in a world full of peace and brotherly love, without hate, greed or violence. Overprotection, however, is just as dangerous as immersing children in a culture of immorality. Experience, both good and bad, is what defines who we are. More often than not, our failures make us better people. Yet our culture is hypersensitive to danger and has a horrible tendency to overdramatize. Just watch the nightly news. At the first hint of trouble, we sound the alert, panic over the "what-ifs," and tighten the protective reins.

We do that in church too. If something goes against tradition, we often run away from it, even if it is helpful and biblical. We forget to open up the Bible to learn about something new instead of running in fear of the unknown. How can we grow in Christ if we're not allowed to experience the ups and downs of life? I don't mean you should run straight into a dangerous situation and see what happens; rather, you should take lessons from your daily successes and failures. Don't shelter yourself or others from situations with possible negative side effects, but, should the worst happen, learn from it. Only through experiences, bad and good, can we mature as individuals and grow in Christ.

Luke 19:1-10

1 He entered Jericho and was passing through.

2 And behold, there was a man named Zacchaeus. He was a chief tax collector and was rich.

3 And he was seeking to see who Jesus was, but on account of the crowd he could not, because he was small in stature.

4 So he ran on ahead and climbed up into a sycamore tree to see him, for he was about to pass that way.

5 And when Jesus came to the place, he looked up and said to him, "Zacchaeus, hurry and come down, for I must stay at your house today."

6 So he hurried and came down and received him joyfully.

7 And when they saw it, they all grumbled, "He has gone in to be the guest of a man who is a sinner."

8 And Zacchaeus stood and said to the Lord, "Behold, Lord, the half of my goods I give to the poor. And if I have defrauded anyone of anything, I restore it fourfold."

9 And Jesus said to him, "Today salvation has come to this house, since he also is a son of Abraham.

10 "For the Son of Man came to seek and to save the lost."

If a baby doesn't struggle to crawl, he or she will never learn to walk. If we don't test ourselves, how will we learn our weaknesses? How can we improve ourselves if we don't know what needs improving? Christ taught us to embrace the many obstacles in life as lessons to build our faith. In difficult times, we question whether God is watching. How can He allow suffering among His faithful? With such questions, however, we grow and reach new levels of belief more profound than anything learned in Bible classes or sermons.

Life is full of obstacles and challenges – some we're capable of handling on our own, and others require outside support. Our forefathers were well aware of this and filled the Bible with helpful stories to guide us through difficulty. Just look at Luke 19. Christ entered Jericho and met a man named Zacchaeus, a chief tax collector of the city and a man of great wealth.

The message of Luke 19 is simple: no obstacle is too great if you commit yourself to living for the Lord. Zacchaeus was immediately judged negatively by Christ's followers because he was wealthy and because the people hated tax collectors. Moreover, Zacchaeus was too short to see Jesus above the crowd. But he did not let these obstacles keep him down. Instead, he climbed a tree just to get a glimpse of the Messiah. More notable was his comment to Jesus about possible, albeit unintentional, defrauding.

Shortness aside, it is remarkable that Zacchaeus would admit to defrauding people, even if it was on accident. We hardly introduce ourselves to new people by admitting our mistakes. We like to gloss over the negative and present only the positive in order to make a good impression; no one wants to be judged by a stranger. Yet this is exactly what Zacchaeus did. He presented himself fairly to Jesus, admitting his mistakes with the assurance that he would correct them fourfold (Luke 19:8). Did Christ chastise him? Punish him? Shun him? Of course not! Christ promised Zacchaeus salvation. It is the sinner, Jesus said, who is in greater need of aid; He had come to save the lost and lead them along the righteous path.

Rocky Roads

Jesus did not abandon Zacchaeus after he admitted his mistake, and neither will He abandon you. But He also will not remove every obstacle from your path. Think back to the time when Christ greeted His disciples while walking across the water (Matthew 14:22-33). Christ had left His disciples to journey across the water alone; He went on a mountain to pray privately. They thought they had seen a ghost when He later appeared to them, walking on the water. They doubted Jesus' ability to save them from the storm. Did Christ banish the inclement weather and save them? No, He forced them to overcome their fears and reached for Peter only when the apostle's faith was at its weakest point: "But when [Peter] saw the wind, he was afraid, and beginning to sink he cried out, 'Lord, save me.' Jesus immediately reached out his hand and took hold of him, saying to him, 'O you of little faith, why did you doubt?'" (vv. 30-31).

Many other passages in the Bible offer comfort when we find ourselves brought down by strife or doubt. In Romans, we are told that suffering ultimately leads to hope: "Not only that, but we rejoice in our sufferings, knowing that suffering produces endurance, and endurance produces character, and character produces hope" (Romans 5:3-4). We learn from our struggles, strengthening our weaknesses so as to be better prepared for future trials. When you are feeling low, do you accept it, or do you hope for something better? The nature of man is to hope, just as it is for us to be tempted to sin. But consider 1 Corinthians 10:13: "No temptation has overtaken you that is not common to man. God is faithful, and he will not let you be tempted beyond your ability, but with the temptation he will also provide the way of escape, that you may be able to endure it." There are many others, but these two passages are the most profound. They remind us that we're not alone. Everyone struggles from time to time; everyone is tempted to stray from the path of righteousness. Sometimes you might lose your way, but if you learn from those experiences, your faith will only get stronger.

Strengthened Faith

Often, when we first learn to ride a bike, we make our parents promise not to let go. But what do they ultimately do? They let go. We usually fall at least once, but this never stops us from getting back on, right? We know that no matter how many times we fall, our parents will always be there to check our injuries and offer comfort. As we grow, we are less likely to have a parent or loved one present to comfort us after our falls, but those with faith are never truly alone. The Lord is always with us, ready to offer comfort and aid if we are strong enough to ask for it.

Zacchaeus did not seek salvation when he climbed the sycamore tree. He only wanted to know "who Jesus was" (Luke 19:3); curiosity brought him before Christ and ultimately to conversion. He was not innocent of wrongdoing, as he freely admitted. But Jesus cared more about Zacchaeus' future than his past. He was willing to repent of his cheating ways and move forward. We should never fear moving on to the future. We should not fear new things or hide from them because we fear failure. Fear is one of the greatest obstacles we face because it can control every aspect of our lives. Fear does funny things to the mind. It clouds judgment and causes people to compromise their morals. We care more about whether people like us than whether *we* should like *them*. Fear causes people to quit, causes friends to be enemies, and kindles distrust when there is no cause for it. Fear can incapacitate us so that we no longer live a full life.

However, we need not fear when we have God on our side. God is stretching out His hand, calling you to climb out of the hole in which Satan is trying to trap you. In that moment, when you finally look up and allow Christ's love to fill you, you will be safe. Your faith will be strengthened tenfold, and your defenses will protect you against Satan's future plots. Everyone goes through a stormy time when they question their faith. Faith is hard, remember, and sometimes we all want that glimmer of light to shine down and explain to us, once and for all, why things are the way they are. But each time you face your fears and God delivers you, your faith will be strengthened.

One of the more popular movie genres involves superheroes: *The Avengers, The Man of Steel, Spider-Man, X-Men*. These movies are popular because we all fantasize about being a hero. These characters save the world, rescue the weak and protect humankind against forces of evil. Superheroes make things peaceful, calm and safe, and we connect with them because we want to control the negative. You might not know it, but you are growing up in a society obsessed with safety. I am not saying safety is a bad thing. Many precautions save lives, but when do precautions become hindrances?

It seems we have a law and special procedure for everything now. We put more padding on our children when they go biking than when riding a horse. This obsession also influences the church. I hear parents refusing to allow their children to go on mission trips to another country because it's too dangerous. Although we are not promised that everything we do for the Lord will be safe, if we ever want to feel like a superhero, we have to take risks for the Lord. A mountain-moving faith is a bold faith.

Instead of dwelling on the obstacles or the struggles, realize that Jesus is waiting for you on the other side. He is waiting with love and compassion as you take those cautious steps toward a stronger faith. You might have been tested and tempted to veer from the path, but He has never left you. He will watch you mature from your experiences, and, should you begin to stumble, He will reach out and encourage you to continue. An interesting fact about fear is that to overcome it, you must first face it. It may take time before you are ready to hop back on your bike after a fall, but when you do, it's with renewed courage and an unmatched sense of triumph. The process will seem agonizing at times, and you might wonder if the struggles will ever end. Don't worry; they will. And when you reach the end of that dark, turbulent tunnel, God will be waiting as He does for all who seek Him and grow in His love.

Discussion Questions

1. What does it mean to "grow in Christ"? How is that accomplished?

2. Was Zacchaeus a bad man for committing mistakes, or was he a good man for owning up to them? When you make a mistake, what is your first reaction?

3. Romans 5:3-5 names the qualities produced by suffering. What are they, and how are they helpful toward building strong faith?

4. In 1 Corinthians 10:13, Paul described God's promised route of escape from temptation. What is your part in overcoming temptation?

5. What are some consequences of allowing fear to take over your mind?

CLIMBING 101

Miscalculations

Robert Frost wrote the poem "The Road Not Taken" with the famous lines, "Two roads diverged in a wood, and I – I took the one less traveled by." These words carry an important message for how to live life to the fullest but are not ideal for safe mountaineering. People who have little experience hiking typically make rookie mistakes. Following trails through difficult terrain is a taxing process, both physically and mentally, which can cause people to look for shortcuts. It seems easier to take the direct route to the top, but this is so often a dangerous mistake. You should always stay on the trail or, if there is no definable trail, follow the markers made of piled stones, or "cairns," that are there to guide you along your way.

A rookie mistake is getting lost on a mountain and continuing to go forward. It is best to backtrack and see where you went wrong, rather than to find yourself even more lost. All too often you will find yourself on a part of the mountain with no option of going up or down. In these circumstances, ignore Frost's advice and take the path most traveled.

8

Faith With Friends

1 Peter 4:1-5

One summer, a group of us were hiking in the Crestone range. There are two peaks in this range that are relatively close together, Crestone Needle and Crestone Peak, both roughly 12 miles from the trailhead to the peak itself. My group decided to start with Crestone Needle on day one, camp down in the **basin**, and then climb Crestone Peak on day two. The weather looked terrible, so we had to hope that it would remain clear during the day; otherwise the hike might not happen. Fortunately, the rain kept away, and we summited the Needle before noon. The rest of the day was to be spent hiking down into the basin and setting up camp. Believe me, after that workout I was looking forward to a night of rest.

My friend Nick, however, wanted us to keep going. He wanted to ascend the Needle and the Peak in one day, which meant an extra seven-mile climb. We had been traveling since midnight the night before and had already climbed more than 3,000 vertical feet. What Nick proposed was a total of 7,000 vertical feet in one day, which would strain even the most seasoned climber. On top of all this, it still looked like rain. I was not excited to be caught on the top of Crestone Peak in a thunderstorm. But Nick, despite these concerns, was adamant that we keep going. I didn't want to go; I wanted to head to camp and sleep. Next thing I knew, however, we were halfway up the next peak with no chance of turning around. I had not said anything about my concerns or my wish to rest, because I didn't want to be the one to chicken out.

After 15 hours of climbing, we stood on the summit of the second peak. Fortunately, the rain never came. By the end, I was proud and exhausted – but mostly exhausted. Although we avoided any accidents, our decision to follow Nick put our lives in danger. I still wonder why I agreed to keep going. There was no reason not to make camp; it would have been the safer option for sure. I talked with Martin, one of my fellow climbers, about how hard the climb was and mentioned how I hadn't wanted to keep going in the first place. Neither had Martin. He had hoped I would speak up and convince Nick we should head down into the basin. I had hoped Martin would say the same thing. Instead, we both went along with the more outspoken member for fear we would look ... what? Weak? Scared? We would still have climbed the second peak, but after our bodies had the rest they needed. The smarter decision was overridden simply because we did not have the courage to say no.

1 Peter 4:1-5

1 Since therefore Christ suffered in the flesh, arm yourselves with the same way of thinking, for whoever has suffered in the flesh has ceased from sin,

2 so as to live for the rest of the time in the flesh no longer for human passions but for the will of God.

3 For the time that is past suffices for doing what the Gentiles want to do, living in sensuality, passions, drunkenness, orgies, drinking parties, and lawless idolatry.

4 With respect to this they are surprised when you do not join them in the same flood of debauchery, and they malign you;

5 but they will give account to him who is ready to judge the living and the dead.

Influence is powerful in faith development. Your faith is either strengthened or weakened by classmates, friends, teachers and family members. As we mature, we develop our personal beliefs based on the good and bad examples they have provided. This is how children approach the complexity of faith. They rely on the wisdom of their elders to guide them down the right path, just as their elders trust in the Lord. Eventually, their beliefs develop and grow as they become better educated and more secure in their own ideas, but they're never free of the opinions of others.

Peter warned against the dangers of conformity. He was all too aware of the pressure his brethren would face from the Gentiles and Jews who were unable to understand or accept the glory of Christ. Early Christians were ridiculed and tormented for their beliefs, but Peter gave them hope. He who follows in the footsteps of Christ is never alone, for he walks with his brothers and sisters in faith. Together, they suffer; together, they triumph because Christ unites them in their faith (1 Peter 4:1-2).

Choosing Our Social Circle

Every day you make choices. Most are harmless, everyday decisions like eating toast instead of a bagel or wearing that blue shirt you like instead of the red one. But then there are the rare and more important choices that have long-term consequences. Television, books and even educational documentaries we watch in school tell us to say no, walk away and not be pressured into doing something we don't want to do. In most instances, this is easier said than done. We are only in school for a short time, but those are important years in our social development when we learn how to communicate and interact with our peers. Moreover, our teen years are when we try to find out who we are and begin to make comparisons between "me" and "everyone else."

Throughout your life, you will notice that we divide society into many social categories. We differentiate people by their wealth, career, education level, hobbies, nationality and religion. People need to feel they belong to a bigger group so as not to feel alone. The world is a large and sometimes intimidating place, and we're very small in comparison. It is understandable that, at times, we feel overwhelmed and a bit lost. We want to know where we fit in. Have you ever lied or pretended to be something you're not just to fit into a group? Have you ever wished you had a different body, better clothes or more money just to hang out with certain people at school? Change is not, in and of itself, a bad thing; change for the wrong reasons, however, is never good.

Social groups greatly affect who we are and what we do. We enter into these miniature communities because we believe we share similarities with the other members. But the risk we all take when we involve ourselves in such groups – though we all do it – is losing a sense of who we are as individuals. The pressure of belonging, just as Peter said, results in mockery if we fail. No one wants to be the object of jokes or rumors. In order to protect ourselves, we do or say things we don't really mean. Look at Peter's denial of Christ. He was faithful to the Lord and stood with Him through many trials, yet after Jesus was arrested, Peter feared being associated with Him. Fear of punishment and isolation drove him to lie and deny the Son of God. But when we choose to please our friends and satisfy our earthly needs, remember we are also choosing not to please God.

There are moments when we must protest against something we know to be wrong: cheating on a test, bullying in school, using drugs or alcohol. We resist speaking up because we fear losing our friends or social status, but does society's opinion matter if it condones something that is so obviously wrong? Peter understood this. He understood the need to belong and the dangers that are presented if we are weak of heart. After all, he had lived through the experience himself. He saw his fellow believers in Christ revert to old, sinful habits, and he sought to save their souls. The early Christians were brave in stepping away from ancient and accepted beliefs for the sake of following and living by something new. They moved into the unknown, sometimes against the wishes of their friends and family. How brave they must have been to stand alone and believe in Christ and His promises when it could have meant persecution and isolation.

However, the people Peter spoke to were never truly alone. Each man, woman and child who accepted Christ belonged to a community of faith. Although they may not have met each other, they knew one another through Christ: "For just as the body is one and has many members, and all the members of the body, though many, are one body, so it is with Christ" (1 Corinthians 12:12). Even when you are feeling misunderstood, alone or lost among those who know you best, you are still a part of God's growing community. Each of us suffers from time to time, as Jesus did before us; but as God was there for His Son, He is here for us too. It is important to remember we are part of something bigger than ourselves. We are part of something greater than how we look or what we own. When you look at your friends, don't focus on their appearance or possessions; look instead to yourself, and ask whether that person will walk along your side on God's path or lead you into darkness.

Living for Christ

I have taken part in teen hiking trips up the fourteeners for many years. On one of our first trips, we had a large group of boys set to climb Yale Peak, which is an eight-mile hike covering more than 14,196 vertical feet. We did not expect all the boys to reach the summit; it was the first climb for many of them. But we wanted to give them the opportunity to try something new, to challenge themselves, because even a short climb is a triumph for first-time hikers. How surprised I was when every single one of them reached the summit that day!

The trip was so successful that we did it again the following year with a new group. We picked a different peak, but it was just as physically demanding as Yale Peak, and the boys were again of varied levels of experience. Based on the previous year, I expected to be surprised again, and I was. Instead of reaching the summit, however, most of the boys turned back at different stages, leaving only a few who reached the top. There was nothing physically wrong with the boys stopping and returning to camp; they just hit their wall of endurance and said enough was enough.

Why, then, did the previous year's group all reach the summit?

I was baffled for a while until I realized a difference in the group dynamic. The first group had motivators, leaders who pushed the others to aim higher. No one wanted to be the first to turn back, to say "I've had enough." The pressure of the group pushed them forward. By the end of the climb, the individual pleasure felt upon reaching the summit was pretty amazing. There were no regrets and no complaints, only a new confidence in ability and endurance.

The second group was composed of different personalities that did not push each other forward. When the first person called it quits, he set a precedent for his fellow climbers. His admission opened the way for others to turn back without fear of being mocked or feeling weaker than their peers. It takes a certain amount of strength to admit you cannot or will not continue and to walk away from the group. The boys who turned around knew their level of tolerance; they didn't try to prove anything. Both groups illustrated the power of social pressure. The first achieved something great through teamwork, motivation and support. The second revealed internal strength of character by knowing their limits, despite the inherent power of the group dynamic. I was equally proud of both groups.

Humans are social creatures. In groups, we are strong and confident and can do wondrous things. However, in groups we can also cause great harm. Peter knew how hard it was for his new brothers in Christ to avoid temptation. He said, "the time that is past suffices for doing what the Gentiles want to do" (1 Peter 4:3). He acknowledged that these new Christians had committed sins but assured them that salvation still awaited anyone who sought it. But in order to continue down the righteous path, they had to separate themselves from their former groups. Otherwise they would be tempted to continue in the sin the Gentiles were doing. Let those sins stay in the past, he explained; pray and be watchful, and God will guide you.

Groups can also bless you, like those in church; they help you along your personal journey of faith. They are your family in Christ and walk the righteous path with you. Being a member of the church, however, does not automatically imply righteous behavior. I have known many people who attend church regularly and are ardent in their belief. Yet when they are outside church, they succumb to the same vices Peter warned his brothers against. Not everyone has the strength to walk away from social pressure, because the fear of becoming an outcast is too terrifying. We are social beings; we want to belong, to fit in and to be part of something bigger than ourselves. This is why people do questionable things and why they hurt themselves or others in the hope to "fit in."

Even though we are social beings, there are times when, as Christians, we have to follow the example of Christ and walk a new path, alone. But even He was not alone for long. His faith and good example brought others to His side. This is what Peter sought to remind others. We are never truly alone because we are all part of a greater community that lives for the Lord. If we stand by our faith, we shall redefine society through individual acts of strength.

Discussion Questions

1. Have you ever allowed the influence of others to put you in a compromising position? Why is the influence of your friends so powerful?

2. Why is the sense of belonging so powerful within us? How does Christ provide a sense of belonging?

3. Can being in the wrong peer group negatively influence your faith? What would you do if your friends ridiculed your beliefs?

4. Who in your life has positively influenced and guided you in the faith? How can you be a better influence on people for Christ?

5. What does being a member of Christ's community mean to you personally?

CLIMBING 101

Teammates

Mountaineering alone is, in general, an ill-advised decision. There is safety in numbers, particularly when there is no cell-phone service for miles and miles. Who will go for help if you become injured? Climbing with another experienced partner provides support and protection against slips and falls, miscalculations and even the stress extreme situations can place on the mind.

There are other reasons not related to safety, however, which make a partner or group more appealing when climbing. You can motivate each other to continue the journey and share resources, like your tent and food. You have someone to back up your stories of danger and feats of daring. You will have someone to whine to on mile 20. More importantly, you will have someone to share in the magnificent glory experienced only upon reaching the summit and an adventure that you will never forget.

9

Faith to Faith

Romans 1:11-17

Recently my family was in town, visiting from Nova Scotia, Canada. Over the last few years, my brother has become interested in visiting Colorado to climb a fourteener. Before their visit, he had trained for more than a year for such a climb. When I had their itinerary, I scouted the area and picked Mount Evans, which is a short drive from Denver and easy to access because of a paved road nearly reaching the top. This is a great mountain for beginners. In fact, about five years ago I climbed it myself. It was a solo trip and relatively safe to hike, but while climbing, I was constantly getting lost. There was an established trail up to the rock ridge marked by **cairns,** or man-made rock piles, but when I first hiked this peak, I ended up all over the place. I could never stay on the proper trail. I was scaling over rock and going places that had no trail whatsoever.

During this last trip with my family, however, I was amazed at my ability to find the cairns so easily. After five years of hiking, I realized how much I had grown as a climber and hiker. Returning to this basic mountain after years of practice, I kept to the main route, saw the cairns in the distance, and never strayed from the trail. How could I have been so blind before? How had I missed so many markers? I didn't have the experience yet to know what to look for or what to do in case I made a mistake. But this last time, with five years of experience and 47 fourteeners to my credit, I navigated Mount Evans with ease.

Experience comes with experience. That's a bit confusing, so let me explain. When I started hiking the Colorado Mountains, I did so with people who also had little experience. Unlike some people who hire guides or experts to introduce them to the sport, we had the blind leading the blind. None of us had any clue about techniques required in the high country, but as we continued climbing together, we grew together. None of us had any extra clues on what to do in a given circumstance: What ledge would support our weight? Is this or that safe to hike over? Although we grew together in our knowledge and confidence, the trials we faced would have been easier if we had acquired someone with more advanced skills to teach us.

Faith works the same way. Supports and guides are present to assist beginners on the path, but they are useless if we do not seek them out. The Bible, our elders and ministers, even our family and brethren, are all there to help instruct us on how to live for Christ. This is the process of expanding "faith to faith." Someone who is strong in the faith mentors someone who is weak. We guide each other so that no one goes without the guidance of a faithful Christian. Young Christians deserve the support of an experienced faith guide to help ensure that they do not get lost on the journey and fall away from the Lord.

Romans 1:11-17

11 For I long to see you, that I may impart to you some spiritual gift to strengthen you –

12 that is, that we may be mutually encouraged by each other's faith, both yours and mine.

13 I do not want you to be unaware, brothers, that I have often intended to come to you (but thus far have been prevented), in order that I may reap some harvest among you as well as among the rest of the Gentiles.

14 I am under obligation both to Greeks and to barbarians, both to the wise and to the foolish.

15 So I am eager to preach the gospel to you also who are in Rome.

16 For I am not ashamed of the gospel, for it is the power of God for salvation to everyone who believes, to the Jew first and also to the Greek.

17 For in it the righteousness of God is revealed from faith for faith, as it is written, "The righteous shall live by faith."

A faith-to-faith experience is not a revolutionary concept. Paul preached this very method to Christians in the first century. He wanted to journey to Rome so he could speak with the Christians there, to teach and strengthen them.

All roads led to Rome. It was the epicenter of the Western world, the capital of an empire encompassing over 3 million square miles and more than 50 million people. Paul's desired trip to Rome was not a random journey or a sightseeing extravaganza. He had already traveled across the breadth of the Roman Empire, leading people to the Lord through His Son, Jesus. Roman Christians, however, were without direct guidance. Christ's apostles had yet to make their way to Rome, leaving Paul as the first to offer his experience in keeping them on the path.

Paul desired to impact the next generation of the faithful, to help these young Christians develop in Christ. He was a warrior for the Lord, a soldier of Christ. His weapon was the Word, and his armor was his faith. He traveled thousands of miles and endured terrible hardships all in order to assist his fellow Christians. His understanding of the importance of this faith-to-faith method allowed him to impact many people.

The need to visit local congregations was vital in the first century because there were no mass media, no bulk production of manuscripts or papyri that could be transported thousands of miles. If you wanted to know God's will, to be educated in the faith, you needed a patron or mentor to pass the message onward. In Romans 11, Paul spoke of the beautiful feet of the evangelist. Why were they beautiful? Because these feet carried the message of salvation to mankind.

Sharing Your Faith

Modern America prides itself on individualism. It promotes choice and opportunity, limiting us only to the reaches of our imagination, but it also blinds us. Pride blinds us. Who needs help when we are free to do as we wish? Who would admit weakness or mistakes when we expect ourselves to be self-sufficient? So many American Christians believe all they need is themselves and a Bible but refuse to be part of the church. They assume they can read the Word of God without explanation, without context. This is a false idea begun by Satan and promoted by modern ideals.

The first act of God, when Adam stood alone in Eden, was to create Eve. Man was not meant to be alone, but in a community. We all enjoy our solitude and time away from the chaos of life, but we also crave human interaction. As a young person, you need others around you to develop your social skills and prepare you for joining society. Similarly, you need to be among those who can assist you along your path to faith. Do not succumb to pride and insist you can do this on your own, because you do not have to. People around you are willing to help. Paul said to the Romans that he was dedicated to everyone: Christian and Gentile, fool and scholar, foreigner and national. He helped anyone who sought to live more fully for Christ and urged others to do the same.

Years ago a group of us were climbing Longs Peak in the Rocky Mountain National Park. Considered a class-three mountain, it was the most difficult mountain we had climbed at the time. Plenty of rock climbing was involved, **vertical rises** that required our hands and feet to ascend to the top. There was also exposure on the trail, places where, if you lost your footing, you could drop over a thousand vertical feet. Going up the mountain was all right, but coming down was a different story. We really felt the steepness of the terrain and the distance to the bottom. Fortunately, another group was attempting the climb and had hired a trained guide to lead them down. Instead of trying to go on my own, I simply followed the experience-led group down the most dangerous part of the peak. It would have been foolish to go on my own when someone was there who could guide me safely through the dangerous portion.

The guide on the mountain was trained to help other climbers. He wanted to help beginning climbers enhance their skills. In his way, he passed experience on to others, just as Paul sought to do in Rome. There was no discrimination, no selection process, merely an open invitation to all who sought to let Christ into their hearts. Paul refused to be prejudiced in his teaching. He knew that to transmit the faith, he had to be invested in the process of communicating it to everyone. As young people beginning your journey through life, you will learn new things every day. Some things will be good; others, bad; some will be helpful; others, not. You will meet people you like and those you do not. And throughout, you will face the trials of daily life: physical, social and mental changes that can be burdensome and wonderful all at once. So why go through it alone?

Adolescence is likely the hardest part of growing up. You're trying to find yourself and distinguish "you" from "them." Having someone mentor you is hardly appealing when you don't know who you are yet. But faith to faith isn't a one-way street. As a teen, you can teach the older generations just as much as they can teach you. People can be intimidated by youth. You are new to the scene but able to understand technology and ideas that your parents and grandparents find utterly foreign. More experienced people provide the tools to help you discover yourself, but you can also give them the opportunity to rediscover themselves. There is no better way to learn than to teach. By accepting guidance, you allow your mentors the chance to learn from you as well. We all need someone from time to time to help guide us through this journey of life and faith. The trail is difficult at times, and no one deserves to walk it alone.

Seeking Open Hearts

On Mount Evans, my mother was scared to death. She hated the hike. It was too steep, too slippery and too dangerous. My brother was fine; so was my father. But my mother was uncomfortable enough that I lingered behind to help her. As we walked along, I noticed two girls hiking ahead of us who had gone off the trail. When they started going farther in the wrong direction, I hurried forward and warned them that they had missed the turn-off for the trail. My mother was shocked that they had strayed because she assumed that because they were climbing the mountain, they must have known what they were doing. But these girls were probably just like me a few years ago – taking to the sport with determination, enthusiasm and inexperience – which made me think of the dangers in choosing a proper guide, specifically when attempting to live for the Lord. A Christian guide needs to be strong in the faith, adhere to the lessons of Christ, and live for Him every day in all that he or she does. In this way, a guide will be righteous and capable of preaching righteousness to others.

In Romans 1:16-17, Paul said that he was "not ashamed of the gospel, for it is the power of God for salvation to everyone who believes. ... For in it the righteousness of God is revealed from faith to faith, as it is written, 'The righteous shall live by faith.'" Faith does not just happen. It is something you learn to develop, something you watch; if you are not paying attention, it will pass you by. Those who live by faith are those who pass it on to others. Paul's faith commanded him to spread its glory and share in the salvation promised by Christ for the righteous. His good works, however, would never have succeeded if his audience had not heard him with open hearts and minds. It is a partnership. A faith-to-faith dynamic requires two parties willing to share and grow in Christ; as Jesus said again and again, "he who has ears, let him hear."

Have any of you played the "telephone" game? Everyone sits in a circle, and the leader whispers a phrase into his neighbor's ear, which is then passed from person to person down the line. When the phrase is returned to the leader, it is usually completely different from how it started. The game is meant to caution us against taking words at face value and acknowledge the frailty of our understanding. The message inevitably changes as it goes around the circle, sometimes with hilarious outcomes. What if we applied this game to most verbal communication between humans? Have we not all been told something, only to repeat it with a slightly different twist? Often, this is not on purpose, just a trick of the brain. The problem arises when we do not seek clarification or when we accept what we have heard at face value. This is passive listening.

Faith requires active listening. The receiver must be open to hearing and understanding the message shared. Elders, preachers, parents – all might be communicating the faith to you, but if your heart is closed to what they say, then you are denying yourself the salvation promised by Christ. If you tune the message out, it will not sink into your heart, and the chain of faith will be broken. Not only should you listen, but you should listen carefully, comparing what you are told to what you read in Scripture. Moreover, we must have the confidence to ask for more and become better educated in the faith and grow in Christ. Only then will we be able to continue Paul's legacy and share the message of Christ with others as he did nearly 2,000 years ago.

Discussion Questions

1. How can elders be spiritual guides for teens? What would you like to see elders doing to help you in your faith?

2. In Romans 1:13-14, name the groups of people Paul felt accountable to when sharing the gospel. How do you feel about people holding you accountable? Is this a biblical concept?

3. How has individualism hurt the Lord's church? Is it possible to balance individualism with faith?

4. As a teen, how can you bless the faith of those who are older than you? What can you share with elders, your parents or your friends?

CLIMBING 101

Signs

Often on the fourteeners, the trail is barely marked. Sometimes it is a path; sometimes it is little more than a trail of rock kicked aside through many years. Often the only way to know the way is by following cairns, but these formations have a tendency to blend into the countless other rocks on the mountain. You can walk right by these formations without even seeing them. Moreover, people can become too enthusiastic about marking the trail, which causes cairns to be placed everywhere and not always correctly. Therefore, you cannot be certain whether or not the cairn is accurate.

No matter how much we refuse to admit it, we are all following in other people's footsteps. You have to be able to trust the path others have created and trust it will lead you down the right path. Unfortunately, we all make miscalculations from time to time. What truly matters, though, is our ability to pick ourselves up, dust ourselves off and begin again following the *right* markers along the *right* path.

10

Unfair Advantage
Matthew 8:5-13

During a trip last summer, we met a young man named Jordan White, who was guiding some clients along a peak that we ourselves were summiting. In the Colorado climbing community, Jordan is famous. When he was 19 years old, he and his father climbed the Bell Cord on Maroon Peak, which is a 45 degree path up the mountain. There was snow on the Cord when Jordan climbed it, but more worrisome was the snowstorm building around him. It blew in quickly, forcing Jordan and his father to scurry down the Cord. The danger of the climb and weather led Jordan's father to lower him down with a rope, but after about 250 feet down, the rope gave out and Jordan fell. He somersaulted down the steep mountain face until finally landing in 9 inches of snow, stained with blood.

After composing himself, Jordan began to look for his father. Following the rope, which was still attached to his harness, he discovered his father, lifeless, in the snow. In order to survive, Jordan forced himself to leave his father's body and drag himself – broken leg and all – back toward the trailhead. He made it three miles but still had three to go. In that spot, he stopped for the night, clinging to life during the cold night. At dawn, he once again embarked on his journey, made it to his car, and called 911. The sheriff's deputy met him on the side of the road and offered to drive him to the hospital, but Jordan figured switching cars was pointless as it would further exhaust him and hurt his leg. Instead, he drove himself.

Before he went into the emergency room, he called his mother. "Papa's dead," he told her. "We had a climbing fall and Papa's dead." His parents had been married for 25 years.

When we met Jordan on that summer's day, we all looked over and at the Bell Cord looming in the distance. It was hard to believe that Jordan was still climbing mountains, let alone in light of such a tragic experience. Jordan, however, accepted that mountains are not fair. They just are.

We live with the assumption that if we treat everyone fairly and act morally, we will be rewarded. Sometimes we are, and sometimes we are not. Moreover, we want others to treat us in a similarly fair way. Sometimes they do, and sometimes they don't. This principle of fairness can also be found in the faith. We come across examples of people who feel at a disadvantage among their spiritual peers. Perhaps your family does not participate in extracurricular activities at church, but your friend's family does. Maybe the people sitting next to you at church are old friends of an elder or the minister. What if your parents are divorced and one of them doesn't attend church anymore, meaning that when you visit that other parent you don't attend either? Your friend, on the other hand, has two parents who attend regularly.

When we see the things that are absent from our lives, we feel cheated. How fair can the world and God be to give others these advantages? What if this one aspect of our lives was different? Would we be different? We might be stronger, happier, better. We might not struggle with faith or doubt ourselves. Have you ever asked what it would be like if you had a better youth group or preacher? What about a better congregation? A better family? Different experiences growing up? All too often we use these disadvantages as excuses. It is easier to justify our lack of faith because of some external factor, rather than our personal weakness. By acknowledging this weakness, however, we will want to try harder, grow stronger and develop ourselves to be better followers of Christ.

Matthew 8:5-13

5 When he had entered Capernaum, a centurion came forward to him, appealing to him,

6 "Lord, my servant is lying paralyzed at home, suffering terribly."

7 And he said to him, "I will come and heal him."

8 But the centurion replied, "Lord, I am not worthy to have you come under my roof, but only say the word, and my servant will be healed.

9 "For I too am a man under authority, with soldiers under me. And I say to one, 'Go,' and he goes, and to another, 'Come,' and he comes, and to my servant, 'Do this,' and he does it."

10 When Jesus heard this, he marveled and said to those who followed him, "Truly, I tell you, with no one in Israel have I found such faith.

11 "I tell you, many will come from east and west and recline at table with Abraham, Isaac, and Jacob in the kingdom of heaven,

12 "while the sons of the kingdom will be thrown into the outer darkness. In that place there will be weeping and gnashing of teeth."

13 And to the centurion Jesus said, "Go; let it be done for you as you have believed." And the servant was healed at that very moment.

The centurion who approached Jesus for aid in Capernaum was not a likely adherent to the faith. First of all, he was a Gentile and a Roman soldier who followed a pagan tradition, not Judaism. Second, his position as a centurion meant that the general Jewish population despised him. Roman soldiers were burdened with the task of collecting taxes from the Jewish temples, money commonly used for pagan purposes. Third, the Gentile population was not Christ's immediate concern. Later in Matthew, Jesus stated that He had come to help the house of Israel first and foremost, not the few Gentiles who saw truth in His teaching (Matthew 15:24). For these reasons, the centurion's request for Christ's assistance was remarkable.

Yet despite his background, the centurion believed in Christ's power and, whether intentionally or not, performed an act of Christian charity. He sought aid for his servant who had assisted him during his mandatory 20 years as a soldier. Despite the likelihood that the man was a slave, the centurion treated him as he would a member of his family, seeking aid when the man was ill. It was a display of humility on the part of the soldier and an acceptance of his limits as both a man and an officer. Because of this acknowledgement, Jesus agreed to help him.

This example shows that it is not always an advantageous position that promotes strong faith. For if his heritage and ethnicity were not enough, the centurion's experience as a soldier would have also proved disadvantageous as far as faith is concerned. War changes people and introduces doubt among even those with the strongest faith. My grandfather was such a man. During World War II, he fought in Europe, and his experiences in the face of constant death and destruction turned him away from his faith. To his dying day, he refused to accept God or Christ. He did not believe in God's very existence. At the end of his life, a minister approached him, hoping to prepare my grandfather's spirit for its passing from this world. My grandfather's words to the preacher were "If you saw what I saw, you would not believe in God too."

It's difficult to imagine what he saw or felt during the war and unfair of us to belittle such an experience. He was so affected by that brief period of his life that he turned away from God. Who has not questioned God's existence in such moments? When we see the brutality of war, the pain of our fellow man, and the unfair suffering of innocents, we wonder how He can allow such things. But, remember, faith is hard. It requires strength and commitment, like that of the centurion, who, despite his position as an enemy of the Jewish people, still accepted the power of Christ and His Father.

Don't Stumble Over the Negative

We already know the centurion was at a distinct disadvantage when he approached Jesus for aid. In the original Greek translation of Matthew, Christ's response stressed the personal pronoun "I" and implied a question rather than a statement: "Shall *I* come and heal him?" In this emphasis, Christ asked what the centurion's opinion was of God's Son and His reported powers. Was it Jesus, an enemy of the empire and a secondary citizen to the Romans, whom this Gentile wanted to heal his servant?

Already the centurion revealed his compassion, wishing his servant to be saved from his ailment. In the first century, slaves were little more than possessions, bought and sold like grain. This one particular Roman, however, overcame cultural stigmas and professed the Christian ideal of loving one's neighbor. He humbled himself further, telling Christ he was not worthy of His presence and thereby expressing his belief in the Son's greatness. He was but one man in a long chain of command, ordering the soldiers under his authority but answering to another higher-ranked officer. He had no true power unless his superiors granted it to him. This form of supplication found favor with Jesus.

What Christ did by asking "Shall *I* come and heal him?" was challenge the centurion's belief. He forced the Roman to commit to his belief. The centurion acknowledged his disadvantage and humbled himself before Jesus by admitting to those elements that would otherwise oppose him to the faith. Christ's question resulted in a strengthening of faith in the Gentile. If we admit to our disadvantages, whether they are in our control or not, we allow ourselves to grow in Christ rather than to become overwhelmed by self-doubt or envy.

In *Unbroken*, author Laura Hillenbrand tells the story of a World War II veteran named Louis Zamperini. After a childhood where he was often getting into trouble, he qualified for track and for the 1936 Berlin Olympics, thereafter enlisting in the U.S. Air Force in 1941. On a search and rescue mission in the Pacific, his plane suffered mechanical problems and crash-landed in the ocean near the Hawaiian Islands. Zamperini and two other crewmates, the only other survivors of the crash, were cast adrift on a life raft, floundering about the ocean for more than a month. They ate raw fish and albatross, drank whatever rainwater they could collect, and fended off sharks. When they finally made it back to land – the Marshall Islands – Japanese forces immediately imprisoned them. From the time of their capture in 1942 until the end of the war in 1945, Zamperini and his fellow inmates were beaten and tortured by their wardens. They survived by sheer will and the camaraderie of fellow prisoners.

Returning home after the war, Zamperini fell in love and married, but his experiences were hardly forgotten. Suffering from post-traumatic stress disorder, he drank heavily and abused his wife while under its influence. Never a religious man, what faith he had was sorely challenged, making his occasional prayers less hopeful, less meaningful. At his wife's encouragement, he attended an evangelical preaching school in 1949 and rediscovered his faith. Like Paul, Zamperini found a new, stronger faith and went out among the masses to preach on Christ's behalf. Was it despite his suffering or because of it that he kindled such a profound faith? If he had never been a prisoner of war in the Pacific, would he have returned to the church afterward? What we might consider a disadvantage proved to be the turning point in his life; the tragic events produced a life lived for Christ.

Is the Grass Always Greener?

Did you know there are only two times in the Gospels where Jesus marveled at something? In Mark 6:6, He marveled at the people of Nazareth, His own people, who refused to believe what He taught them. And He marveled in Matthew 8:10 at the impressive show of faith by the Roman centurion. No son of Israel had exhibited as much faith as this Gentile. Christ, who was more concerned with His people than their pagan counterparts, exclaimed that many more like the centurion would come to the faith, their belief stronger than those born into it. The centurion's faith shows that ethnicity, heredity and culture matter little when weighing the strength of belief. Instead, how you practice the faith, how you treat your fellow man, and how you live each day of your life for Christ are what define you.

In Matthew 8, we are taught that it does not matter what we have but what we do with it. The children of Israel were God's chosen people (Deuteronomy 14:2), who first worshiped the one true Lord and passed His laws to their children. Christ Himself was a Jew and lived by their laws even as He spoke the words passed to Him by His Father. Yet the Jews ultimately spurned Christ and refused His message of salvation. In contrast, this soldier of Rome with no background in Judaism or its culture was able to see Jesus for who He was: the Son of God. This was the principle Jesus emphasized:

anyone who desires to know Jesus – regardless of race, religious origins or heredity – might dine with Christ and His apostles in heaven. Those who deny Christ, despite many opportunities offered them to grow in faith, will be left in the outer darkness.

We all have difficult situations in life, but they should never be an excuse to give up on God. None of us approach the Lord with the same experience or background. It is easy to play the victim. It is easier still to complain about everyone else's advantages and the unfairness of it all. But it is what we do with our disadvantages that defines us. Will we quit and pity our lost chances, or will we dust ourselves off and prepare to try again? Focusing on the negative aspects of our lives only hinders our success in the future. Would the centurion have approached Christ for help if he thought only of the reasons why he should not?

Faith is not developed through equal opportunity but from the goodness of one's heart. There will always be someone with a better background in the church or someone with better preachers, parents or elders. Each of these advantages, however, is worthless if you do not have faith and continue to develop it in Christ. Just as the soldier believed and was blessed, so too will you be blessed.

Discussion Questions

1. Is Jesus always fair to people? Why, or why not?

2. Do you believe that church leadership should always be fair, and if so, how do you measure this fairness?

3. Does growing up with Christian parents and attending church services regularly give you an advantage in the faith? Why, or why not?

4. We all deal with suffering at some level. How can we keep suffering from damaging our faith?

5. In observing teens who have a strong faith and those who have turned their backs on God, what would you say are the key differences between the two groups?

CLIMBING 101

Odds

Reinhold Messner, a world-famous mountaineer and author, once said, "Mountains are not fair or unfair, they are just dangerous." This statement is resoundingly accurate. No matter how prepared you are or how cautious you are when climbing, at the end of the day, anything can and will happen.

I subscribe to a website called 14ers.com, where I have connected with various people also interested in the hobby of hiking. In the last six years, however, some of these varied and amazing people I have been in contact with have died in the mountains. Often these individuals were not attempting anything extremely dangerous, just simple hikes they had done many times before. It was the indifference of the mountain that caused them to fall. A rock might have slipped or a storm appeared – perhaps the cold came in too quickly or they became lost on a poorly marked trail. In the end, these individuals died alone in the unforgiving terrain. In the mountains, you never know when your time is up. All you can do is prepare yourself for any and all circumstances and follow the right markers to the top.

11

Lustful Climbing

1 Timothy 6:9-10, 17-19

When you get ready to go out – whether for the night, the weekend or an extended vacation – you create a mental checklist. Do I have my keys? my wallet? license? tickets? We prepare ourselves for what may come and hope we have accounted for all possibilities. When I go mountain climbing, I do the same thing. Is my gear all set? Do I have my first-aid kit, and is it stocked with everything I might need? I remember to bring a compass and a map because even the most experienced climber can get lost. I also bring a pocket-sized mirror.

Before you imagine me checking my hair while scaling a rock face, know that the mirror is an important survival tool. If you become stranded on the mountain, a mirror can help you start fires by reflecting sunlight into dried grass. The fire will keep you warm and protect you from wild animals. Moreover, the fire or even the mirror itself can act as a beacon to rescuers. In densely forested areas or on mountainsides, a fire might be the only visible sign from the air that can lead search teams to you. Using such a simple tool, you can reveal your position quickly and save yourself from a life or death situation.

1 Timothy 6:9-10, 17-19

9 But those who desire to be rich fall into temptation, into a snare, into many senseless and harmful desires that plunge people into ruin and destruction.

10 For the love of money is a root of all kinds of evils. It is through this craving that some have wandered away from the faith and pierced themselves with many pangs. ...

17 As for the rich in this present age, charge them not to be haughty, nor to set their hopes on the uncertainty of riches, but on God, who richly provides us with everything to enjoy.

18 They are to do good, to be rich in good works, to be generous and ready to share,

19 thus storing up treasure for themselves as a good foundation for the future, so that they may take hold of that which is truly life.

Like the simple mirror, we sometimes take things for granted, thinking they serve a single purpose and no other. Take money for example. Financial security is fundamentally important to most Americans. We are raised in a money-conscious society that is obsessed with making it, saving it, spending it and sometimes losing it. We idolize those who have it because Americans want stuff and lots of it. And this is not necessarily a bad thing – so long as the desire does not rule our actions, as Paul warned about in 1 Timothy 6:9-10. Money presents the opportunity to help others, but it also paves the slippery slope to destruction. Just as the mirror can serve our vanity or salvation, so too can wealth enable or disable the Lord's work.

Human history has taught us that money equals power. The richest men made the rules and upheld them regardless of public opinion. In the waning years of monarchical power, America sought independence through wars to ensure that it would never come under English control again. Centuries later, American television, newspapers and magazines are obsessed with British royal weddings and subsequent babies. Why? We see prestige in wealth. As children we dream of being movie stars, sports icons or famous musicians because we desire the glory of fame and the comfort wealth would provide. This association pushes us to idolize famous people until we can name every actor in a current sitcom but not key government officials who define the laws by which we live.

There is a strong temptation to believe that wealth equals God's favor. This attitude is deeply rooted in America. During tragic events and political campaigns, people often look to celebrities for words of wisdom. We attribute a certain amount of respect to the rich because these individuals are wealthy. But money is not a sign of God's blessing. Someone with great wealth is not automatically more spiritual than someone who is extremely poor. Spirituality is not judged by the size of the pocketbook, but by one's faithfulness to the mission of the Lord.

The Snare of Wealth

As Christians, we are expected to follow Christ's warnings against the corruption of wealth (Matthew 19:16-24). Worldly possessions threaten to blind us to other, more important matters and trick us into judging someone based on his or her bank account. Christ warned that "the cares of the world and the deceitfulness of riches choke the word, and it proves unfruitful" (13:22). Wealth is worthless if it is allowed to cloud our faith and serve selfish purposes.

Paul warned Timothy about the desire to be rich and the danger it was to the soul. Wealth itself is harmless, but the lust for it is destructive: "But those who desire to be rich fall into temptation, into a snare, into many senseless and harmful desires that plunge people into ruin and destruction" (1 Timothy 6:9). Throughout the Bible, many have deep spirituality as well as great wealth; the two are not exclusive. A problem arises, however, when the need for wealth suppresses spiritual growth. Christ warned: "No one can serve two masters, for either he will hate the one and love the other, or he will be devoted to the one and despise the other. You cannot serve God and money" (Matthew 6:24).

Paul referred to wealth as a snare, an unforeseen obstacle that could grab onto you and hold fast. No matter how hard you try to escape, the trap tightens, keeping you prisoner. Wealth brings with it jealousy, envy, rage and even hatred. Any time you envy someone's clothes or possessions, you fuel the wickedness Christ warned against because you're blinded by what you see on the outside. The desire for wealth ensnares us with greed, draining our soul of all that is good until we're no better than the wickedest sinner. These are the consequences of lusting after wealth. Such desire weakens our soul, allowing other vices to intrude. Greed, like other sins, obscures our priorities. It dazzles and taunts us with possibilities while danger lurks beneath. You cannot focus on how you interact with others when you care only for acquiring something new; you cannot grow in the Lord and seek salvation if you think only of your next purchase.

How do we avoid such a snare in our modern, capitalistic society? Everywhere we look, advertisements are luring us to buy new products or upgrade our old ones. Our culture has always emphasized the ability to rise from rags to riches. To avoid this seductive power of riches, we need to stay focused on the mission of the church. The church seeks to spread the gospel of Christ. You need to develop the habit of giving early in life before greed and selfishness can take root. If you learn to place value on souls, instead of all the value on your money, you can avoid this pitfall of danger. Souls are the most valuable item on earth.

Distorted Images

Have you ever been to a funhouse or seen one on television? They usually have a special room full of mirrors that distort your reflection: three heads, no neck, a squished torso and giant eyes. They are humorous, warped pictures meant to make us laugh. But what would happen if we stopped thinking these images were ridiculous and began to believe them as genuine? What if we began to hate ourselves because we thought we actually looked like our reflection in those funhouse mirrors?

The desire for wealth can distort reality just as easily as those mirrors. We begin to see ourselves through what we own, what we earn or what we wear. As teenagers, we struggle to find our identity in a very large world and adapt our look so we can fit in with what we wish ourselves to be. We have all seen examples of someone trying to fit in with a group – changing his or her clothes, hair, speech and even beliefs in order to belong to a group that is "right" or "better." This is completely normal because we find ourselves, ultimately, through trial and error. Still, your image is only a small piece of who you are, and if you focus too hard on the image, you risk losing sight of the person behind it.

Wealth can allow us to change our image, but it can never change who we are. We idolize athletes, musicians and actors because of their glamorous lifestyle, which is only achievable with an extremely high income. We listen to politicians, our nation's leaders, who present one face to the world but hide their true selves. They use their position, sometimes unwittingly, to lead us astray: "For, speaking loud boasts of folly, they entice by sensual passions of the flesh those who are barely escaping from those who live in error (2 Peter 2:18). It is important to remember that these people – who garner power through money, fame and stirring speeches – are human and, therefore, fallible. We must remember to ask ourselves how much we really know about these media icons. How much of what we hear is true? How much is false?

The misfortune of our species is that we are more concerned with self-promotion than with the enrichment of all. Wealth often leads to power, and with power, often comes arrogance, pride and fear. Satan tempts us through money with what *could be*, just as he tempted Adam and Eve. Instead of faith in God and themselves, Adam and Eve ate of the forbidden fruit and were expelled from the Garden of Eden. In their greed, they sinned against God; it is a lesson to heed because through our need for bigger, better and newer possessions, we also risk succumbing to temptations that will harm our spiritual health.

The Riches of the Righteous

Paul was well aware of Satan's use of wealth to ensnare us and lead us from God. He urged us instead to view riches through the eyes of the Lord (1 Timothy 6:17-19). Paul emphasized the many positive opportunities that might be obtained if a person were to use his wealth for the good of all. In giving to the less fortunate, we strengthen our souls with righteousness and, perhaps more importantly, "set the believers an example in speech, in conduct, in love, in faith, in purity" (4:12).

Not long ago I was visiting a congregation in Texas, where I was asked to share my conversion story. I told the members that I was baptized in Texas at a little congregation in an even smaller town. Despite its size, the congregation supported me through school as I sought to become a minister. It was a true example, I told them, of the power of giving and sharing. The congregation could have kept their charity for themselves, but they looked beyond themselves and supported me so that I might, in turn, share Christ's teachings with the world.

After I told my personal story, a woman approached me and asked if I knew her father. I did because he was the very man who had supported me as I trained to be a preacher. If not for her father, I might not be preaching at all, and for that, I thanked her. What a legacy for his children! She listened to a young preacher stand before a congregation earnestly wishing to help others and able to do so only because her father looked beyond his own desires. He created a foundation for the future and changed my life for the better. All that I accomplish, any good that God allows me to do, is because of this stranger's father. It is a lesson neither she nor I will forget: a small act of charity can affect the lives of many.

In my youth, I was fortunate enough to know someone who gave selflessly in my support. Many are not so lucky, for wealth all too often leads to vice rather than charity. How often do you hear of a celebrity being mixed up in some sort of scandal? What about the morality of these media icons? Miley Cyrus, at the 2013 Video Music Awards, is a prime example of losing one's path. No longer a child star, she flaunted her body in a rebellious struggle to find herself without thought to those impressionable fans who want to imitate her. She is a lost soul, blinded by position and wealth and without the support of moral teachers. For her, wealth is a burden: it distorts reality and blinds her from discovering her true self.

This has happened to all too many child stars. Few escape the lights of stardom, fame and fortune without being tainted by its immorality. Justin Bieber is another young celebrity snared by the allure of wealth and fame. Reckless driving, substance abuse, vandalism: he claims to be a Christian with a close relationship with

Jesus, but what he does contradicts what he says. His actions are not examples of good spiritual deeds but sins that the entire world can see and that God will judge.

What Paul taught in 1 Timothy is to beware becoming a victim of wealth. Those who are blessed with fortune ought to bless others through generosity and charity. He urged his listeners not to forget that this life is temporary; in the hereafter, we will be judged, and our souls will either be sent to their eternal reward or everlasting damnation. In this way, we need to realize it is not an entirely selfless revolution upon which Paul asked us to embark. We are fighting for our spiritual salvation as well as the greater glory of the Lord; we need to look to the richness of our soul, rather than that of our wallet. In America, we are fortunate to have the freedom to grow and better ourselves financially, but we also have the duty to help others. Paul appealed to everyone to make a moral and righteous impact with individual wealth, for we are leaving a legacy in the Lord, and our investments in the kingdom will outlive us all.

Discussion Questions

1. How important is it to spend time in self reflection? Do you believe you can have an accurate impression of yourself?

2. In 1 Timothy 6:9-10, what are some of the negative consequences of desiring to be rich? Do you see this happening in America today?

3. Another reference in the Bible that warns against the dangers of money and wealth is Matthew 13:22. What do riches choke according to this verse? Is there a way to balance wealth and faith?

4. How many childhood stars have you watched go from beloved idol to sinful example? Do you think wealth alone led to this transformation?

CLIMBING 101

Checklists

Have you ever attempted to go grocery shopping without a list? It is chaos. Pandemonium. You revisit the same aisle four or five times, buying multiple items you didn't need in the first place, all while forgetting to grab the milk, which was why you went shopping in the first place. It is exhausting to say the least. This is when a checklist becomes invaluable. It not only organizes your mind, it limits the time and energy wasted on running around like a crazed fool.

Checklists in mountaineering are even more important because they can save you from a life or death situation. I have a specific list I follow each and every time I spend a day hiking a fourteener.

1. water
2. warm clothing
3. backpack
4. food
5. hiking boots
6. hat and gloves (it's amazing how often people forget these)
7. sunscreen
8. sunglasses
9. camera
10. toilet paper (a vital necessity)
11. compass, first-aid kit and matches
12. a pocked-sized mirror
13. extra socks
14. and one doughnut (I never forget the doughnut)

Each of these items is critical to a successful hike; successful in that I reach the summit and survive the trek back down.

12

Backpacking Faith
James 2:18-24

At the Castle Rock church, we have a large group of people who love to go camping. They load up the camper and drive to a local campsite, where they enjoy one another's company and the beauty of nature. Each time they return, they report to the congregation how wonderful the trip was, how nice it was to get away, and how amazing the camping experience was. I am always happy to hear how fun it was and to know that people within the congregation are strengthening their faith. But is it really camping? They have electricity, beds and a kitchen all in the camper as well as modern conveniences like heat and air conditioning. They go into nature without really leaving civilization behind. They are "RVing," as I like to call it, not camping in the traditional sense.

While nothing is wrong with RVing, I prefer the old-fashioned tradition where everything I need to survive is in a pack on my back, where I cook over a fire I started myself, and where I sleep beneath the stars. Each person approaches camping in a different way. But if we all have differing definitions of what camping involves, then how do we know what we are talking about? We can never hope to understand each other if we cannot agree on a simple thing like vocabulary. Faith is no different. If everybody has a different understanding of what God expects, then how are we to know whether we are on the right path? When we say we have faith, what does that entail?

Faith is more than saying "I believe." It is the commitment to worship the Lord in all you say and do. True faith involves pure living and good deeds that spread the Lord's love to all mankind. Camping, quite simply, involves a return to nature with the barest amount of necessities to keep you alive. It is a form of pure living in which your body and mind focus on a single purpose: survival. RVing does not place the same demands on you. It does not force you to give yourself wholly to the experience. People tend to seek out the easiest path, hoping for a limited amount of inconvenience. It's no different with faith. God requires us to prove our faith, to produce tangible examples that we're obedient to His will. He wants to know that we're improving and growing in our faith, not saying we believe when we really don't.

James 2:18-24

18 But someone will say, "You have faith and I have works." Show me your faith apart from your works, and I will show you my faith by my works.

19 You believe that God is one; you do well. Even the demons believe – and shudder!

20 Do you want to be shown, you foolish person, that faith apart from works is useless?

21 Was not Abraham our father justified by works when he offered up his son Isaac on the altar?

22 You see that faith was active along with his works, and faith was completed by his works;

23 and the Scripture was fulfilled that says, "Abraham believed God, and it was counted to him as righteousness" – and he was called a friend of God.

24 You see that a person is justified by works and not by faith alone.

When you say you have faith, what do you mean? Do you attend church regularly? Do you give to charity from time to time? Do you tell others you believe in God, but don't actively seek Him out? We all have an interpretation of faith – what it involves and how to express it. Our belief is tempered by the people in our lives and by our culture. You will meet countless people in your school, workplace and community who adhere to most Christian ideals. Millions of Americans believe Jesus is the Christ, but few attend church, the simplest of Christian acts. You can say you believe in Jesus; you can shout it from the mountains until it echoes around the world. But words aren't enough. You need to show your faith in good works; you need to put your faith into action.

James preached the importance of balancing faith with works, stating that we cannot simply claim to believe but must prove ourselves to the Lord (James 2:18-20). The intensity of what he wrote is like a verbal slap in the face. Anyone can believe in God; after all, demons believe in Him and know Jesus to be His Son. Their actions, however, prove a lack of faith. They actively seek to turn mankind against the Savior. This is what James warned us about: belief does not promise faith or understanding. He used Abraham's willingness to sacrifice Isaac as proof of faith (vv. 21-24).

Abraham was willing to give up what mattered most, and because of this, God knew his faith was true and spared him the loss. This example is extreme, but James used it not only to prove the importance of our actions but also to reveal how easy his listeners have it. Today, our faith is tested by simpler, day-to-day activities: how we treat our fellow man, our humility, our works of charity toward the less fortunate. These are the deeds by which we are judged because they reveal the strength of our trust in Christ and all He taught.

Good Works

When you go camping in an RV, you aren't making many sacrifices. There is little to no "roughing it" when you have electricity, indoor plumbing and television. If this is the experience you want to have, that is fine, but you cannot call it camping – maybe lite camping but not real, backpacking camping. Likewise, you can believe in Christ, but without good works, you cannot really call it faith. I was on a train in Durango, Colo., once when I passed by an RV park that was right next to a main road, and McDonald's was only a 5-minute drive away. A sign at the park advertised free Wi-Fi and cable television. Call me old-fashioned, but this doesn't seem like camping. If you can get to a fast-food restaurant in 5 minutes, you really have not immersed yourself into nature. What made this truly funny was that the train I was on with a friend of mine was returning us to civilization from the great outdoors. We had just spent a few days in the wilderness, 12 miles from the nearest town or road – camping in the traditional sense.

My point is this: do not be confused by vocabulary. There are key differences between people who "camp" in an RV and those who "camp" in a sleeping bag under the stars. Just so, there are major differences between people who *say* they have faith and people who *demonstrate* faith. There needs to be proof of your commitment. Think of any math test you have taken in school. How many times has your teacher said "Show your work"? Perhaps you had the correct answer but lost points because you did not show your work. Without you showing your work, your teacher has no idea whether you understood the subject or memorized test answers and cheated. You can tell everyone you meet that you believe in God and are one of His faithful, but how can we measure your sincerity if you cannot show us your faith by your good works?

So what are these good works? What can you do to prove your faith and strengthen it? What is it that Jesus is really asking of you? Jesus taught His followers many lessons about keeping the faith and finding salvation. We must attend church regularly (Luke 4:16; Acts 18:4) and improve our faith with study and prayer (Matthew 6:6; 1 Thessalonians 5:17; Acts 17:11). We must aid those who are less fortunate by showing charity (Matthew 6:1-4; Mark 8:36; Luke 12:15; 1 Timothy 6:9-10) and participate in services to better the lives of all (Mark 10:42-45; Galatians 5:13). Action is what ties all these elements together. We can proclaim Jesus as Lord until our voices grow hoarse, but it will mean nothing if we do not *act* according to His teaching (James 2:18-24; Matthew 7:21-23; Luke 6:46-49).

Good Faith

Works are the true test of a mature faith. Those with a weak faith see works as a burden, not a blessing. They complain about having to go to worship service, saying it is too inconvenient or that there is not enough reward for the effort involved. It is characteristic of humankind to seek to simplify a given chore in order to make it easier. We seek efficiency rather than quality. We are annoyed with giving a few hours a week to church and faith while we waste countless hours playing video games, watching movies or spending money on frivolous objects. So, I have to ask, which is more likely to please God: giving your time to help others and be an example of good faith or being obsessed with playing video games?

James assures us that "'Abraham believed God, and it was counted to him as righteousness' – and he was called a friend of God. You see that a person is justified by works and not by faith alone" (James 2:23-24). Abraham had true faith, proved by his willingness to sacrifice one of the most important people in his life at God's command. This is as far from a "feel-good" religion as I can imagine. How long had Abraham and Sarah waited for a child and then later were commanded to sacrifice him to God? Abraham was not simply losing his son but was willingly taking the boy's life. Talk about emotional trauma. What else could have given him the strength to accept this loss but faith? We are asked to do so little in comparison to prove our trust in the Lord. Christ sacrificed Himself so that we might attain salvation. In return, He demanded only that we continue His work by giving aid to the poor and sick, improving ourselves with study and prayer, and spreading God's love to all mankind.

The Friend of God

When you go camping, you typically go in a group. More than one person assures safety in the wilderness should inclement weather approach or any accidents occur. Removed from civilization, you rely on one another to see you through the experience. If you filter water for drinking, you make sure there is enough for all on the trip, not only yourself. If you cook supper, you make enough to share. You share the responsibility of pitching the tent, carrying supplies, and holding the map. You share because you are all in this together, and your actions show this to your companions. They will better trust you if you pull your own weight, and they will be more willing to help you should you need it.

Abraham was a friend of God because he was willing to give up his son as a sacrifice. His actions proved his faith in the Lord, who returned this trust by stopping him from killing his son. No one wants to help the selfish jerk who refuses to lift a finger but takes a share of the pie anyway. When you serve the Lord, you might give up a lot, but you know through faith that He will always be there for you. He is the ultimate camping companion, prepared to share His supplies and support as you travel into the wilderness of life.

Discussion Questions

1. When you say you have faith, what exactly do you mean? How do you prove it? What actions do you take to demonstrate obedient faith?

2. James said even the demons believe in God. Does this mean they are saved? Why, or why not?

3. Abraham is considered the father of the faithful. What did he have to do to prove to God that he was completely obedient to the Lord? Could he have demonstrated his faith without works? Why, or why not?

4. What is the problem with misunderstanding the definition of "faith"? How can you assure that you understand "faith" correctly? How can you share the true meaning with others?

5. What does it mean to be called "a friend of God"? What can you do to be God's friend?

CLIMBING 101

Knowledge

Never forget this rule: after securing a good camping spot with flat ground and good tree cover (in case of lightning) take all of your food, put it in a bag and hang it over a high branch. Bears will sniff it out; if that food is on the ground, it is fair game. You cannot just set food up in a tree; black bears can climb trees after all. It needs to hang over a branch where the bear cannot reach it. The last thing you want to do is keep food in your tent or else you will have an unwelcome guest or two visiting in the middle of the night.

Camping requires understanding. You need to know the terrain and the wildlife in order to avoid unnecessary risks. More importantly, you need to respect it. Just as the mountain can be unforgiving, so can the wilderness at ground level. Prepare your checklists, be wary of the weather and remember that you are not in control of the natural world around you. All you can do is be ready for any and all situations.

13

By Faith

Hebrews 11:23-29

In my office in Castle Rock, Colo., there are two books that I keep on display. Both are very special to me in many ways. The first book is *No Shortcuts to the Top*, a first edition, autographed copy of Ed Viesturs' autobiography. This was the book that made me want to start climbing mountains. After I moved to Colorado I started to read Viesturs' book and when I finished, I figured I should go climb one of those fourteeners nearby. This book started my journey in the mountains, and I have never looked back.

The other special book is the autobiography of Sir Edmund Hillary, *View from the Summit*. Hillary was the first man to summit Mount Everest, the tallest mountain in the world. My copy is also a first edition, and it is autographed. Hillary and Viesturs were men who accomplished something phenomenal: they conquered mountains. They were simple, ordinary men who accomplished the extraordinary and, in having done so, inspire me every day to push forward in finishing my goals and conquering my mountains.

Only rare individuals receive the prestige of an internationally published biography. For most of us, our public memory will be stored in the simplicity of an obituary, a brief testament to our achievements in life. How do we sum up an entire life in one small paragraph? What do we want to remember about that person? We often mention family, such as the survivors, and the place of birth. If the deceased served the country as a civil servant or in the military, it is common to include any such distinctions or actions. We use those brief moments to celebrate a life, not to dwell on misdeeds or failures. Have you ever read an obituary that recalled someone's arrest record or history of drug abuse? No, we gloss over the negative with bland details because no one is comfortable with speaking ill of the dead, despite the wickedness they might have perpetrated in life.

Hebrews 11:23-29

23 By faith Moses, when he was born, was hidden for three months by his parents, because they saw that the child was beautiful, and they were not afraid of the king's edict.

24 By faith Moses, when he was grown up, refused to be called the son of Pharaoh's daughter,

25 choosing rather to be mistreated with the people of God than to enjoy the fleeting pleasures of sin.

26 He considered the reproach of Christ greater wealth than the treasures of Egypt, for he was looking to the reward.

27 By faith he left Egypt, not being afraid of the anger of the king, for he endured as seeing him who is invisible.

28 By faith he kept the Passover and sprinkled the blood, so that the Destroyer of the firstborn might not touch them.

29 By faith the people crossed the Red Sea as on dry land, but the Egyptians, when they attempted to do the same, were drowned.

When writing an obituary, you want to highlight an individual's most important contributions. But how do you know what those are? What are the important elements that define a life well-lived? For a Christian, God's commandments are what define a good life and one destined to be rewarded in the hereafter. If we abide by His laws, by faith, we compose a spiritual biography worthy of publication. It will serve as an example to others, guiding them along Christ's path because they will see in you a pattern of success rewarded by God.

The author of Hebrews recorded such spiritual successes. He recalled biblical figures who abided by God's laws and trusted in Him to lead them toward salvation. These brief references focus on how the individuals lived by faith and explain what "living by faith" means (Hebrews 11:1-3). Basically, the author of Hebrews explained that faith should be a part of your daily existence. One of the examples he used to convey this is the life of Moses. Most of us probably know the story of the baby who was placed in a basket by his mother in order to save his life (Exodus 1:22; 2:1-4). We know he was found and adopted by Pharaoh's daughter, becoming the foster brother of Pharaoh's heir (vv. 5-10). What we easily forget is that in this position, Moses would have had everything: power, wealth and sustenance. He would have wanted for nothing for the rest of his life. When he saw the injustice done to one of the Hebrews, though, he did not stand idly by and watch the man being abused. Moses chose to fight for the faith and its people, refusing "to be called the son of Pharaoh's daughter, choosing rather to be mistreated with the people of God than to enjoy the fleeting pleasures of sin. He considered the reproach of Christ greater wealth than the treasures of Egypt, for he was looking to the reward" (Hebrews 11:24-26).

Five times in Hebrews 11:23-29, the author explained that Moses lived and was rewarded *by faith*. *By faith* he was hidden as a baby (v. 23). *By faith* he refused Pharaoh's kinship (v. 24). *By faith* he left Egypt (v. 27), kept Passover (v. 28), and crossed the Red Sea (v. 29). In the face of exile and death, Moses lived each moment dedicated to faith because he believed in the end reward. His experiences are a great example of living by faith and for the Lord, regardless of the obstacles that tempted him to doubt.

Live by Example

The author of Hebrews explained that "faith is the assurance of things hoped for, the conviction of things not seen" (Hebrews 11:1). Faith demands that we set aside all preconceived notions and give our trust to something we cannot see or prove. We are challenged not only by our doubts and misconceptions but also by a modern society that stresses the secular over the religious. What we need to

Matthew W. Morine

do is emulate Moses, Abraham, Noah and other holy figures of the Bible, all of whom were tested by God and found worthy of His grace. We are given the deeds of their lives so we can understand the strength of their individual faith and its power to overcome all obstacles. Just as a modern biography will record the achievements of Lincoln or Gandhi, the Bible shares the long legacy of the faithful.

When we're young, we often don't look to distant, biblical figures to inspire us. Instead, we expect our elders to set the pattern of behavior. Parents, siblings, teachers and ministers: their actions inform us what is right and wrong. We imitate because this is how we learn. What happens when we don't have the proper role model? A church-organized youth group is a wonderful way to communicate with people your own age, to share experiences that help you all grow in the Lord. Such a program, however, requires someone with experience to guide it down the correct path and develop faith. Even so, the group's time together is limited to a few hours here and there. A community- or church-operated organization can only do so much to help with the doubts and questions so common in the young. What happens when you go home? What about the time you spend at school or with your friends? Do the people in your life promote faith development or expect the church to do it for them?

Your peer group will have a huge impact on your spiritual life. Think about your friends; is there anyone that is inspiring you to grow in your faith? Is there a peer that is holding you accountable to Christian standards? If you look around at your closest friends, is this a group that is helping you grow in Christ or holding you back from Christ? Are the people in your youth group excited to participate in the life of the congregation or do these individual treat service in the church like a burden? Look for those people that inspire you to grow spiritually.

Live With Hope

The author of Hebrews told us not only to lead by example but also to put greater value in our actions than in the opinions of others. This is the key to Hebrews as a whole, for it was written to reassure the doubtful of Christ's role as the Messiah. See how Moses forsook the pleasures of the Pharaoh, the book exclaims. See how,

122

by faith, he wandered in exile but found his true home in heaven. We are all wandering blind from time to time, but what separates the faithful from the faithless is hope. We hope in something better: in salvation and the eternal glory promised by God. Thus, we look to our actions as stepping-stones leading to that end; they can either lift us up or make us stumble.

When Moses' mother set him in the basket, she was not sending him to be raised by another. Her selfless act might have saved him from death at Pharaoh's hand, but what about the dangers of the world? Wild animals, turbulent weather and the cruelty of men abound. She cast her baby into a chaotic world, but believed, in doing so, he would be saved. It was her hope and faith in God that gave her the strength to let go and trust that He would see her child to safety. When Moses grew up, the story of his mother's refusing to allow him to die could have inspired boldness in him. Thus, when he faced Pharaoh, the Red Sea, and exile in the desert, he did not cower in fear. *By faith* he led his people forward because he learned from the example of his mother and others who trusted in God and acted according to His will.

How confident must Moses have been to lead so many? How sure was he of his own faith and God's greatness? His people followed him into exile because of hope in something better. I don't know about you, but I would have to be very impressed by someone to willingly leave everything familiar behind and follow him into the wilderness. Trust isn't an easy concept, whether it's in someone else or your own convictions. We have to remember, however, that we aren't alone in our struggles. Those who have gone before us had their own obstacles to surmount. Moses questioned God's commands, asking why he was chosen to go to Pharaoh and even begging for someone else to go instead (Exodus 4:10-13). Fear and doubt find each of us from time to time, but we must remember what God told Moses: "I will be with you" (3:12). Despite Moses' fear, he held onto hope and spread it to others because he knew God would be with them always.

Live by Faith

Like all parents, I want my children to be successful. This includes being well-educated and having successful careers in the future.

Nothing, however, is more important to me than my children's faith and continued triumph in Christ, even after I'm gone. I know this won't happen just because I bring them to Bible class or because I worship with them each Sunday morning. The greatest gift I can provide for my children is to live a bold faith for them, to make my life an example of living for Christ. Years ago, I left Nova Scotia, Canada, to train as a preacher. I left all that was familiar to me – friends, family and culture – and moved to a city where I was very much alone. I had no money, only a single suitcase, and the clothes on my back. Was this a crazy decision? Maybe, but it was done by faith. I put myself in the hands of the Lord and trusted totally in Him.

Looking back to this personal moment of bold faith, I'm filled with God's love. He didn't forsake me, but kept me strong on my blind journey. These are the moments I want my children and others to cherish about my life after I'm gone. But, remember, faith is not only lived in these big, bold moments. Faith is also lived in the little things, the seemingly unimportant moments of our lives. Very few people achieve a monumental accomplishment like a Nobel Prize or an Oscar, but this doesn't mean that what we do every day has no impact.

Humor me for a moment, and imagine a day in your life. Try yesterday. What did you do after waking up? Make a mental list of everything you can remember, including the most trivial activities like putting on your shoes. Now think of all the people you talked to, saw, passed, smiled at; now think about how many people saw you. How many people saw you doing your ordinary, everyday activities? Whether you realize it or not, you made an impact. From how we look to how we speak to what we do, nothing goes unnoticed. If we *live* by faith, it will show in our actions; if we *act* in faith, we will set an example for everyone we meet.

The men and women of the Bible did amazing things against terrible odds. Living by faith, they "conquered kingdoms, enforced justice, obtained promises, stopped the mouths of lions, quenched the power of fire, escaped the edge of the sword, were made strong out of weakness, became mighty in war, put foreign armies to flight" (Hebrews 11:33-34). They were heroes of the faith, warriors for God in the extreme. In comparison, our efforts seem trivial, don't they? Perhaps what we do isn't as grand as leading a mass exodus, but every day you live by faith, you fight one more battle for God. Each day you imitate the life of Christ, you set an example for all you pass. Each time you go into the world and share the words of Jesus, treat your fellow man as brothers and sisters, and live humbly and righteously, you are glorifying God.

And remember that the men and women of faith were not only concerned with living right themselves but also with leading others to the light. They were evangelists of the Word of God, and this is the commitment the Lord will recall at judgment. He won't care what you owned or who you knew; He will judge you because of your actions, good and bad, because these deeds will be the measure of your faith. Right now you're young, beginning on the path of life with a world of opportunity before you. The path won't be easy; indeed, at times it will seem torturous and long. Remember, God is with you, walking at your side; He is your unseen but ever-present support. If we live by faith, by His Word, then we will be rewarded in His kingdom. So, I ask you this one question again: how do you want to be remembered?

Discussion Questions

1. What would you consider to be your greatest accomplishment thus far? What would you consider to be your greatest mistake?

2. In Hebrews 11:23-29, how many times did the author use the phrase "by faith"? What does it mean to live "by faith"?

3. What could you and your family be doing to show a stronger example of faith in the home?

4. Who do you know who has lived or lives by faith? What has that person done to make you believe he or she is faithful?

5. How do you want to be remembered at the end of your life? What will your spiritual legacy be?

CLIMBING 101

The Extraordinary

In Sir Edmund Hillary's book, *View from the Summit*, only the first part concerns his climbing adventures, while the rest highlights his humanitarian work. After becoming famous for being the first man to summit Mount Everest, he traveled back to Nepal to give back to the local people. For the majority of his life, he used his fame to bless the poor nation. Instead of living in luxury, he lived poorly in the Sherpa communities to build schools and hospitals and to provide a better way of life for these people. He was treated like a hero but lived as a servant so he could fill the needs of others less fortunate than himself. He gave up glory so that he could bless others. The most famous mountaineer of all time, the first-ever conqueror of the world's highest peak, chose to mimic Christ's humility and generosity: the greatest of all feats for the righteous to achieve.

Conclusion

The first time I ever climbed a mountain, I was terrified and filled with exhilaration. Never before had I relied so heavily on the strength of my body and mind. Although I was with a group, each step I took was a solitary journey to my end goal; I had to make myself go forward, push harder, and swallow my doubts because if I didn't, no one else would.

Hiking is an adventure; so is faith. The two go surprisingly well together because great accomplishments require work and perseverance in order to reach long-term goals – whether that goal is a class-five peak or the ultimate summit of heaven. Success isn't instantaneous. In a world focused more than ever on instant gratification, this can be a hard concept to understand and accept. We expect success quickly and easily, like a quick level-up in a video game. But faith is a lifelong journey. At times you will look down from the top of the mountain at the wonders below and marvel at your achievements. At other times, you will be trapped in the valley at the foot of the mountain, unable to shake the weights holding you to the ground. These are the worst moments because they seem to never end, but when they do – and they will – your freedom to climb new mountains and greater heights will be all the sweeter.

To have mountain-moving faith, you must develop it through hard work and dedication. Satan is doing everything in his power to stop you from progressing in your faith. He is hoping to side-track you while you're young and innocent so that you won't be a positive force for good later in life. If Satan can cause you to fall away from the church early on, he has one less soldier to fight in the future.

The key is to stay faithful. Stay strong in your commitment to the Lord, and He won't let you stand alone. We are never alone in faith. Millions of Christians in the world are living by faith and seeking salvation. Individually, we might struggle and falter; individually, we might doubt and question God's existence and benevolence. As a people, however, we are strong. The American dollar bears the phrase "E Pluribus Unum": "Out of Many, One." Although this refers to the American people, it's an apt description of Christians the world over.

The early church was a haven for like-minded individuals who followed the teachings of Christ in a time when it was dangerous to do so. They found a new, church-based family to support them and help the young religion grow. You never have to live faithfully by yourself. Even if your family doesn't go to church or refuses to partake in extracurricular church activities, that doesn't mean there is no support base for your faith. Your church family understands what it feels like to be alone while in a room full of people. It is in Christ's teaching, however, to care for one another and offer support, for we are all His brothers and sisters: "For whoever does the will of my Father in heaven is my brother and sister and mother" (Matthew 12:50).

Take these lessons, put on the gear of faith, and face the world with its many trials and tribulations. Use your friends to help you on your journey, but remember to stand beside them should they begin to stumble and fall. Most importantly, test your faith. Don't sit idly and avoid experiences because they seem too challenging. Your footing will not always be secure, and, at times, you might lose your way. But remember God will be at your side, ready to lift you up should you fall. He is there now, waiting and watching in excited anticipation to see your belief mature and lead you closer to the reward of heaven.

God is ready to see you move mountains.

Climbing Glossary

Words defined here are bolded in the text on the first usage.

Alpinist – a mountaineer with great skill and ability to climb the Alps or other high mountains

Anchored – a way of attaching the climber to the object being climbed (e.g. ice or rock) in order to prevent a fall

Ascend – to hike or climb in an upward direction

Basin – a wide, depressed area in which the rock layers all incline toward a central area

Belay – to lower someone or something down a steep area of a trail with a rope; also refers to the anchoring of climbers to each other to protect against falling

Cairn – a mound of rough stones built as a memorial or landmark

Chimney – a natural geologic formation wherein high, almost parallel rock walls create a valley or cleft leading to a higher location

Core temperature – the temperature at which our bodies are meant to operate

Couloir – a narrow gully or fissure in mountainous terrain with a typically steep gradient

Crampon – a device attached to boots to improve traction and mobility when climbing on snow and ice; also used for travel across glaciers, snow and ice fields, ascending snow slopes, and scaling ice-covered rock

Crevasse – a deep, narrow opening or crack in an area of thick ice or rock

Descend – the process of hiking back down a mountain

Downgrade – the downward slope of a trail or mountain path; levels of steepness vary for each downgrade

Drop-off – a cliff on a path that can measure between a few hundred or a few thousand feet

Exposure – the empty space below or next to a climber

Gradient – the steepness of a path, trail or mountain

Handhold – a natural ledge, fissure, or protuberance in the mountainside grabbed with the hands to assist in climbing or hiking

Ledge – a narrow stretch of rock on a mountain path; can be less then a foot in width and might have exposure on one or both sides

Ledge system – a ledge that you walk on with steep vertical drops on one or both sides; mostly where the trail narrows

Microspike – Like crampons, microspikes use smaller spikes to provide traction on icy sections of a trail. These spikes or teeth are typically less than an inch in diameter, while a crampon's teeth measure over an inch.

Rock face – the natural rocky formation on a hiking trail; often has a vertical wall of sheer rock, as well as a variety of other gradients

Range – the section of a mountain within a specific geographic area

Rappel – the act or method of moving down a steep incline by using a rope to ensure safety

Scale – to climb up or over

Snow bridge – the natural phenomenon in which snow melts around a creek or stream, but a section of snow remains, forming a bridge for hikers over the water

Summit – (n.) the top of a mountain; (v.) the act of reaching the top of a mountain

Trailhead – the beginning of a trail

Vertical rise – a section of trail so steep that you must resort to rock climbing

CPSIA information can be obtained
at www.ICGtesting.com
Printed in the USA
LVOW04s1412311015
460449LV00004B/6/P